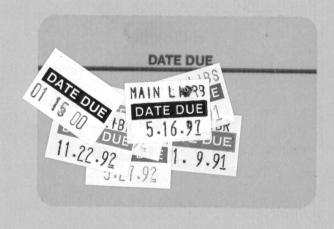

100 EUROPEAN DRAWINGS

in The Metropolitan Museum of Art

100 EUROPEAN DRAWINGS IN THE METROPOLITAN MUSEUM OF ART

Jacob Bean CURATOR OF DRAWINGS

The Metropolitan Museum of Art, (NEW YORK, N. Y.)

Distributed by New York Graphic Society, Greenwich, Connecticut

TABLE OF CONTENTS

FOREWORD

Drawings have a more intimate character than any other form of artistic expression. Often they represent an artist's first thoughts, hastily and spontaneously noted on the paper. They reveal his self-assurance or his hesitancy in the search for a solution that makes a reality of his first idea. They enable us, in a sense, to participate in the artist's act of creation.

The collecting of drawings was long the province of artists themselves. The Florentine Vasari formed one of the first sizable and systematic collections of drawings, and his example was followed by Rembrandt, Rubens, Lely, Reynolds, and Lawrence. Great European museums—the Uffizi, the Louvre, the Berlin Museum, and the British Museum—have old and important collections of drawings. In America public interest in drawings is a fairly recent development; our public collections have short histories. That of the Metropolitan Museum is one of the oldest in the country, and this is due to the foresight of Cornelius Vanderbilt. The initial nucleus of the collection, given by Mr. Vanderbilt in 1880, has been slowly enriched by purchase, gift, and bequest. We owe much to the generosity of many donors and to the foresight of the Museum's curators of paintings, who until recently were responsible for our drawings collection.

The installation of the Blumenthal Patio from Vélez Blanco will now provide a fine exhibition space in which our constantly growing collection of drawings can be exhibited. The arcaded loggias of the Patio are a setting perfectly suited to close-hand inspection of framed drawings. Parts of the permanent collection will be shown, as well as periodic exhibitions of exceptional interest. Students will have access to the recently completed drawings study room in the Thomas J. Watson Library. The most modern methods of storage and air conditioning have been used in new vaults to assure the preservation of the drawings.

In 1960 an independent Department of Drawings was established with Jacob Bean in charge. Under his curatorship many important new acquisitions have been made that greatly strengthen our collection. From the finest of our drawings he has made here a selection that testifies to their range and quality.

JAMES J. RORIMER
Director

INTRODUCTION

In 1880, ten years after the incorporation of the Metropolitan Museum, Cornelius Vanderbilt purchased in Florence and presented to the Museum a collection of 670 "Old Master" drawings. Framed and labeled with the optimistic attributions that accompanied them from Italy, a good many of these drawings were shortly afterward put on public view. This exhibition must have struck a new and European note in New York, reminding the well-traveled of the galleries lined with drawings at the Uffizi and the Louvre, and introducing the novice to a form of artistic expression that until then had been only occasionally appreciated in America. The exhibition of the Vanderbilt drawings seems to have been the first full-scale presentation of European drawings in an American museum, and the time must have been ripe. Exceptional undergraduates already had drawings on their walls; Verena Tarrant in Henry James's *The Bostonians* had visited the rooms at Harvard of the young Henry Burrage, of whom ever so much was thought in New York, and who "collected beautiful things, pictures and antiques and objects that he sent for to Europe on purpose. . . . He had intaglios and Spanish altar-cloths and drawings by the old masters."

Earlier in the century there had been precedents for such collecting. James Bowdoin III, our minister plenipotentiary to the court of Spain and later associate minister to France, had in the course of his travels acquired a group of drawings, which he presented in 1811 to Bowdoin College, in Brunswick, Maine. This small collection of 142 drawings contains a fine mountain landscape by Pieter Brueghel the Elder and a complete representation of the limited stylistic range of a Roman follower of Carlo Maratti, Pietro di Pietri. Considerably more encyclopedic, at least in the range of the attributions, was a group of some four hundred drawings brought together by Joseph Green Cogswell, first Superintendent of the Astor Library, who had traveled abroad with George Ticknor and studied at Göttingen in 1817. Cogswell's collection, which contained interesting seventeenth century drawings and sheets hopefully attributed to Dürer, Watteau, and Boucher, was sold at auction in London in 1938 but returned to America and is now in the California Palace of the Legion of Honor.

The group of drawings purchased by Vanderbilt for the Metropolitan in 1880 had been assembled and sold by James Jackson Jarves, for a very brief period American vice-consul at Florence. Jarves, a fascinating and quixotic figure, had begun his career as a rather unsuccessful Yankee businessman and politician in Hawaii, and ended as a passionate *marchand-amateur* in Florence. From Ruskinian experiments in theoretical writing on the fine arts he had pushed on to collecting on a large scale. At a time when Italian painting of the early fifteenth century was coming into fashion he had acquired a number of such pictures, some of them of considerable importance, as we can judge from those purchased from Jarves by Yale University in 1871.[1]

---

[1] Jarves's collections have been discussed by Albert TenEyck Gardner, *Metropolitan Museum of Art Bulletin,* April 1947, pp. 215–220, and by Francis Steegmuller, *The Two Lives of James Jackson Jarves,* New Haven, 1951.

The introduction to an undated checklist of the Vanderbilt drawings, published by the Metropolitan Museum shortly after 1892, says that the collection was begun in the latter part of the eighteenth century "by Count Maggiori, of Bologna, a learned scholar and connoisseur, and a member of the Academy of Sciences in that city. It has gradually been increased by additions from the celebrated collections of Signor Marietta, Professor Angelini, Doctor Guastalla and Mr. James Jackson Jarves, our Vice-Consul at Florence." The introduction adds, with commendable prudence, "The attributions of authorship are by former owners." Signor Marietta, Professor Angelini, and Doctor Guastalla are otherwise hardly known in the annals of collecting, but drawings that belonged to Alessandro Maggiori can be identified by autograph inscriptions recording the place and date of purchase.[2] Curiously enough, very few of the Jarves-Vanderbilt drawings bear such inscriptions, and Maggiori's name may have been used by Jarves to give particular luster to the provenance at the time of the sale. Drawings that once belonged to Maggiori can be found in several American collections, and they show him to have been a collector partial to average examples of the work of his near-contemporaries in Italy. An exception that proves the rule is a splendid drawing by Vincenzo Catena from Maggiori's collection that now belongs to Janos Scholz.

Pollaiuolo, Mantegna, Michelangelo, Raphael, Andrea del Sarto, Correggio, Parmigianino—a galaxy of the brightest names in the history of Italian draughtsmanship—figure on the early checklist of the Vanderbilt drawings. In 1887, 181 drawings given to the Museum by the painter Cephas G. Thompson were added to the public exhibition. Both these collections were composed almost entirely of Italian drawings, and both, unfortunately, were largely made up of works that seem now to us of little historical or artistic interest. Almost without exception the pretentious attributions they carried have proved indefensible, though both collections contain good examples of the work of minor masters.

By 1906 the weaknesses of the Museum's large permanent exhibition of drawings had become apparent to the Trustees. On the urgent recommendation of J. Pierpont Morgan, then President of the Museum, Roger Fry had come that year from England to accept the post of Curator of Paintings, and he was immediately authorized to remove the drawings collection from public view and to undertake the reclassification of the material. Aided by Bryson Burroughs, then Assistant Curator, and Frank Jewett Mather, later professor at Princeton University, he discarded the grandiloquent attributions that brought discredit to so many of the drawings and arranged them by school and century to form a study collection that could be of service to the public.

Fry was an exceptionally gifted connoisseur with a sharp and imaginative eye, and he opened at the Metropolitan an era of systematic purchase. Indeed, it was with this purpose in mind that the Trustees had invited him to New York. He was, of course, primarily concerned with the Museum's collection of European paintings, but from the beginning of his brief tenure he recommended the acquisition of drawings, and the Museum's first purchases in this field were made at his suggestion. Curator in 1906–1907, he continued after his return to London to act as agent for the Museum until 1910. Through Fry the Metropolitan obtained on the English market in these years some fine drawings, excellent examples of the work of Amico Aspertini (pl. 9), Gillot (pl. 55), Oudry (pl. 57), Cuyp (pl. 90), Gains-

[2] See Frits Lugt, *Les Marques de collections de dessins et d'estampes. Supplément,* The Hague, 1956, no. 3005b.

borough (pl. 98), and J. R. Cozens (pl. 99). One of the Leonardo and one of the Guercino drawings illustrated in this volume (pls. 4 and 30, respectively) are among these early purchases. About the Leonardo Head of an Old Man, Fry, who had bought the drawing for £110 "with a very stunning Jordaens thrown in," wrote in 1909 to Bryson Burroughs, his successor as Curator of Paintings: "I wired to you that I have secured the Leonardo. I think it is a great *coup,* though I don't know whether people in New York are interested enough yet in drawings to realize its rarity and importance."

People here did realize its rarity and importance, and in 1917 the Museum, on the recommendation of Burroughs, purchased in New York two more drawings by Leonardo (pls. 3, 5), sheets of remarkable quality and interest that had once belonged to the Anglo-American painter Thomas Sully. This same year was marked by the purchase in London of a small group of drawings that added particular distinction to our collection. The drawings assembled in the eighteenth century by the Earls of Pembroke and Montgomery had been removed from the library at Wilton House and put up for auction at Sotheby's. Burroughs urged that the Metropolitan make an effort to obtain a number of pieces from this splendid collection. The Museum's bids proved adequate on all but two of the lots of its choice, and seventeen drawings, which reached New York only at the end of World War I, were acquired. The Parri Spinelli (pl. 2), the three Correggios (pls. 16–18), and the Primaticcio (pl. 22) illustrated here reveal the importance of this purchase. Then Burroughs wisely recommended that the Museum participate in two important auctions held in Paris in 1919, and the collection was enriched by ten Degas drawings purchased at the sale of the contents of the artist's studio (pls. 74–76) and two drawings by Ingres (pl. 64) that figured in the François Flameng sale.

In 1924 John Singer Sargent informed the Museum that the widow of the Spanish landscape painter Aureliano de Beruete wished to sell the magnificent Michelangelo drawing (pl. 10) that had been the principal ornament of her husband's collection. In the same year the purchase of the drawing was satisfactorily negotiated in Madrid by Burroughs, who was continuing with discernment the purchase policy inaugurated by Roger Fry. Then, fifty years after the founding gift of drawings from Cornelius Vanderbilt, the H. O. Havemeyer Collection came to the Metropolitan Museum as the bequest of Mrs. Havemeyer. The splendor of the pictures and large pastels in this bequest has tended to overshadow the Havemeyers' gift of sixty-two drawings. Their exceptional quality should be insisted upon here. The gift included seven drawings by Rembrandt (pls. 87–89), two fine water colors by Daumier (pls. 70, 71), twenty-five drawings by Barye (pl. 67), and excellent examples of Guys and Millet.

In 1935 an album of fifty drawings by Goya belonging to the Spanish painter Mariano Fortuny y de Madrazo was shown in the Goya exhibition at the Bibliothèque Nationale in Paris. It was rumored that the drawings could be purchased; a quick decision had to be taken, and funds made immediately available to face serious international competition. George Blumenthal, then President of the Museum, carried out the negotiations, which brought to New York the finest group of Goya drawings (pls. 92–95) outside Madrid. Harry B. Wehle, then Curator of Paintings, published the remarkable series in 1938. Mr. Blumenthal was also instrumental in obtaining for the Metropolitan the collection of the

Marquis de Biron, a French *amateur* who by 1937, at the age of eighty-three, was living in retirement in Geneva. Biron possessed an extraordinary series of drawings by Giambattista and Domenico Tiepolo and a large group of drawings by Francesco Guardi. In 1914 some of these drawings had been put on the auction block in Paris, but, presumably disappointed by bidding that failed to come up to his expectations, Biron had bought many of them back. In 1937 the Metropolitan purchased from Biron 176 drawings and nine paintings, retaining for the Museum 105 drawings and four paintings. The Biron drawings by Giambattista Tiepolo at the Metropolitan (pls. 40–43) constitute perhaps the most sumptuous group of designs by this artist in any collection, public or private, and the Guardi drawings, too (pls. 46, 48), are of the greatest importance. A number of fine French drawings (pls. 56, 60, 63) were also included in this acquisition. Between the Goya purchase of 1935 and that of the Biron drawings in 1937 stands the London sale of the Henry Oppenheimer Collection in 1936. The Museum unfortunately obtained only five drawings on this occasion, but the Filippino Lippi sheet of studies (pl. 6) then acquired is a fine example of fifteenth century Florentine draughtsmanship. The celebrated metalpoint portrait head by Fouquet (pl. 51), the most hotly disputed drawing in the sale, was, happily, acquired by the Museum thirteen years later, in 1949.

Harry B. Wehle and his successor as Curator of European Paintings, Theodore Rousseau, continued the policy of selective acquisition and recommended to the Trustees of the Museum the purchase of a series of important drawings. Sheets by Jacopo della Quercia (pl. 1), Carpaccio (pl. 7), Parmigianino (pl. 20), Rubens (pl. 81), Canaletto (pls. 44, 45), Clodion (pl. 61), Manet (pl. 73), and Picasso (pl. 97) were added to our collection. These acquisitions were made possible by the donations that have given purchase funds to the Museum. The income from the bequest of Jacob Rogers has played a particularly providential role, making possible the purchase of fifty-five drawings illustrated in this book. In the same years the Museum's collection was increased by significant gifts. In 1949 the Alfred Stieglitz bequest brought postimpressionist, fauve, and cubist drawings (pls. 50, 96), strengthening our collection in contemporary fields that had been somewhat neglected. Most of these drawings had figured in pioneering exhibitions at Stieglitz's New York gallery, "291," and some of them had been exhibited in the Armory Show of 1913. The Stieglitz bequest came through the exercise of a power of appointment granted to his wife, Georgia O'Keeffe. Fine drawings by Ingres (pl. 65) were included in the bequest of Grace Rainey Rogers, and that of Stephen C. Clark brought us an exceptional portrait by Seurat (pl. 78); gifts from Harold Hochschild (pls. 47, 82) and from Robert Lehman (pl. 91) are reproduced in this volume, and they stand witness to the importance of the drawings the Metropolitan has received from public-spirited collectors.

The Drawings Department is now installed in new quarters with an exhibition gallery in the Thomas J. Watson Library. Since 1960, when the department was set up as a separate curatorial division, a particularly concentrated effort has been made to enrich our holdings. Several hundred drawings have entered the collection, and thirty-three of these are illustrated here. They range from sheets already well known to students of European draughtsmanship, such as the Parmigianino studies for the Steccata (pl. 21) or Ingres's study for the drapery of Stratonice (pl. 66), to fine yet little known examples that have only recently re-

[12]

appeared, such as De Gheyn's Witches' Sabbath (pl. 85) or Perino del Vaga's design for a fresco (pl. 19). The beautiful double-faced sheet by Raphael (pls. 11, 12), acquired in London in 1964, is the most recent purchase recorded in this volume. The Museum's collection of European drawings is by now eighty-five years old, and from the original Vanderbilt gift of 670 it has grown to include more than 2,600 drawings. This quantitative increase, thanks to the early impetus of Roger Fry, has been paralleled by an increase in the quality and importance of the collection, and in spite of the ever greater rarity of fine drawings on the international market, we are confident that our collection will continue to grow.

This volume replaces two albums of collotype reproductions of European drawings, published by the Museum in 1942 and 1943 but out of print for a number of years. The present publication reproduces sixty-eight drawings that did not appear in the earlier albums, and includes many of the most important drawings acquired in the last twenty-one years. A chronological order within each national school has been adopted, the date or approximate date of the artist's birth determining his place in the sequence of the reproductions. In the case of the most celebrated, often published drawings in the collection, a selective bibliography, limited to essential references, rather than an exhaustive listing is supplied. The list of exhibitions has been confined to important manifestations commemorated in descriptive catalogues. Collectors' marks that appear on the drawings are listed under provenance, and not in the technical description of the sheet. The selection of drawings has been dictated by a desire to reflect the character of our collection at the present stage of its growth; the Italian and French schools are overwhelmingly predominant both in this volume and in the collection, while the Northern schools are represented by a limited number of examples.

The author would like to express his gratitude to Linda Boyer and Gay Patterson Lord for devoted assistance in the preparation of this volume and to Denis Mahon, K. E. Maison, A. E. Popham, and Walter Vitzthum for advice on particular points.

JACOB BEAN

LIST OF WORKS CITED
IN AN ABBREVIATED FORM

Adhémar, *Daumier*
Jean Adhémar, *Honoré Daumier,* Paris, 1954.

Adhémar, *Daumier. Dessins*
Jean Adhémar, *Daumier. Dessins et aquarelles,* Paris, n.d.

Alazard, *Ingres*
Jean Alazard, *Ingres et l'Ingrisme,* Paris, 1950.

Barr, *Picasso*
Alfred H. Barr, Jr., *Picasso. Fifty Years of his Art,* New York, 1946.

Bartsch
Adam Bartsch, *Le Peintre graveur,* 21 vols., Vienna, 1803–1821.

Benesch
Otto Benesch, *The Drawings of Rembrandt,* 6 vols., London, 1954–1957.

Benesch, *Disegni Veneti*
Otto Benesch, *Disegni veneti dell'Albertina di Vienna,* Venice, 1961.

Benesch, *Selected Drawings*
Otto Benesch, *Rembrandt. Selected Drawings,* 2 vols., London, 1947.

Benesch, *Venetian Drawings*
Otto Benesch, *Venetian Drawings of the Eighteenth Century in America,* New York, 1947.

Berenson, 1903
Bernard Berenson, *The Drawings of the Florentine Painters,* 2 vols., London, 1903.

Berenson, 1938
Bernard Berenson, *The Drawings of the Florentine Painters,* amplified ed., 3 vols., Chicago, 1938.

Berenson, 1961
Bernard Berenson, *I Disegni dei pittori fiorentini,* 3 vols., Milan, 1961.

Bodmer, *Leonardo*
Heinrich Bodmer, *Leonardo. Des Meisters Gemälde und Zeichnungen,* Stuttgart, 1931.

Byam Shaw, *Guardi*
J. Byam Shaw, *The Drawings of Francesco Guardi,* London, 1951.

Carderera, *Gazette des Beaux-Arts*
Valentín Carderera, "Les Dessins de Goya," *Gazette des Beaux-Arts,* VII, 1860, pp. 222–227.

Clark, *Leonardo*
Kenneth Clark, *Leonardo da Vinci, an Account of his Development as an Artist,* 2nd ed., Cambridge, 1952.

Commissione Vinciana
I Manoscritti e i disegni di Leonardo da Vinci pubblicati dalla Reale Commissione Vinciana. Disegni, ed. Adolfo Venturi, 4 vols., Rome, 1928–1936.

Constable, *Canaletto*
W. G. Constable, *Canaletto, Giovanni Antonio Canal, 1697–1768,* 2 vols., Oxford, 1962.

Escholier, *Daumier*
Raymond Escholier, *Daumier,* Paris, 1923.

Fischel
Oskar Fischel, *Raphaels Zeichnungen,* 8 portfolios with text, Berlin, 1913–1941.

Freedberg, *Parmigianino*
  Sydney J. Freedberg, *Parmigianino. His Works in Painting,* Cambridge, Massachusetts, 1950.

Fuchs, *Daumier*
  Eduard Fuchs, *Der Maler Daumier,* Munich, 1927.

Fuchs, *Daumier. Supplement*
  Eduard Fuchs, *Der Maler Daumier. Nachtrag-Supplement,* Munich, 1930.

De Hauke, *Seurat*
  C. M. de Hauke, *Seurat et son oeuvre,* 2 vols., Paris, 1961.

Heaton-Sessions, *Art Bulletin*
  Charlotte Heaton-Sessions, "Drawings Attributed to Correggio at the Metropolitan Museum of Art," *Art Bulletin,* XXXVI, no. 3, September 1954.

Herbert, *Seurat's Drawings*
  Robert L. Herbert, *Seurat's Drawings,* New York, 1963.

Heydenreich, *Leonardo*
  Ludwig H. Heydenreich, *Leonardo da Vinci,* 2 vols., New York, 1954.

Ivins, *The Unseen Rembrandt*
  William M. Ivins, *The Unseen Rembrandt,* New York, 1942.

Klossowski, *Daumier*
  Erich Klossowski, *Honoré Daumier,* Munich, 1923.

Lippmann, *Rembrandt*
  F. Lippmann, with the assistance of W. Bode, Sidney Colvin, F. Seymour Haden, and J. P. Heseltine, *Original Drawings by Rembrandt Harmensz. van Rijn,* first series, Part II, London and Berlin, 1890.

Lugt
  Frits Lugt, *Les Marques de collections de dessins et d'estampes . . . ,* Amsterdam 1921; *Supplément,* The Hague, 1956.

Metropolitan Museum, *European Drawings*
  Metropolitan Museum of Art, *European Drawings from the Collections of the Metropolitan Museum of Art,*
    I, *Italian Drawings,* New York, 1942.
    II, *Flemish, Dutch, German, Spanish, French, and British Drawings,* New York, 1943.

Mongan, *One Hundred Drawings*
  Agnes Mongan, *One Hundred Master Drawings,* Cambridge, Massachusetts, 1949.

Morassi, 1955
  Antonio Morassi, *The Paintings of Giambattista Tiepolo,* London, 1955.

Morassi, 1962
  Antonio Morassi, *A Complete Catalogue of the Paintings of G. B. Tiepolo,* London, 1962.

Parker, *Ashmolean Catalogue,* II
  K. T. Parker, *Catalogue of the Drawings in the Ashmolean Museum,* II, *Italian Schools,* Oxford, 1956.

Popham, *Correggio's Drawings*
  A. E. Popham, *Correggio's Drawings,* London, 1957.

Popham, *Leonardo*
  A. E. Popham, *The Drawings of Leonardo da Vinci,* 2nd ed., London, 1949.

Popp, *Leonardo*
  Anny E. Popp, *Leonardo da Vinci. Zeichnungen,* Munich, 1928.

Populus, *Gillot*
  Bernard Populus, *Claude Gillot. Catalogue de l'oeuvre gravé,* Paris, 1930.

Ricci, *Correggio*
  Corrado Ricci, *Correggio,* London and New York, 1930.

Rich, *Degas*
  Daniel Catton Rich, *Degas,* New York, 1951.

Robaut, *Delacroix*
  Alfred Robaut, *L'Oeuvre complet d'Eugène Delacroix,* Paris, 1885.

Rosenthal, *Daumier*
Léon Rosenthal, *Daumier,* Paris, n.d.

Seligman, *Seurat*
Germain Seligman, *The Drawings of Georges Seurat,* New York, 1947.

Sérullaz, *Mémorial*
Maurice Sérullaz, *Mémorial de l'exposition Eugène Delacroix . . . organisée au Musée du Louvre,* Paris, 1963.

Shoolman and Slatkin, *French Drawings*
Regina Shoolman and Charles E. Slatkin, *Six Centuries of French Master Drawings in America,* New York, 1950.

Sterling, *French Paintings*
Charles Sterling, *The Metropolitan Museum of Art. A Catalogue of French Paintings, XV– XVIII Centuries,* Cambridge, Massachusetts, 1955.

Stoll, *Goya. Dessins*
Robert T. Stoll, *Goya. Dessins,* Paris, n.d.

Strong, *Wilton House Drawings*
S. Arthur Strong, *Reproductions in Facsimile of Drawings by the Old Masters in the Collection of the Earl of Pembroke and Montgomery at Wilton House,* London, 1900.

Sturge Moore, *Correggio*
T. Sturge Moore, *Correggio,* London, 1906.

Suida, *Leonardo*
Wilhelm Suida, *Leonardo und sein Kreis,* Munich, 1929.

Tietze, *European Master Drawings*
Hans Tietze, *European Master Drawings in the United States,* New York, 1947.

Tietze, *Venetian Drawings*
Hans Tietze and E. Tietze-Conrat, *The Drawings of the Venetian Painters in the 15th and 16th Centuries,* New York, 1944.

Valentiner, *Metropolitan Museum Studies,* III
W. R. Valentiner, *Rembrandt Drawings in the Havemeyer Collection* ("Metropolitan Museum Studies," III), New York, 1930–1931.

Vasari Society
The *Vasari Society for the Reproduction of Drawings by Old Masters,* first series, 10 vols., London, 1905–1915.

Venturi
Adolfo Venturi, *Storia dell'arte italiana,* 11 vols., Milan, 1901–1939.

Wehle, *Fifty Drawings by Goya*
Harry B. Wehle, *Fifty Drawings by Francisco Goya* ("The Metropolitan Museum of Art Papers," no. 7), New York, 1938.

Wildenstein, *Ingres*
Georges Wildenstein, *Ingres,* London, 1954.

Zervos, *Picasso*
Christian Zervos, *Pablo Picasso,*
 II, Part 1, *Oeuvres de 1906 à 1912,* Paris, 1942.
 II, Part 2, *Oeuvres de 1912 à 1917,* Paris, 1942.

1OO EUROPEAN DRAWINGS

in The Metropolitan Museum of Art

JACOPO DELLA QUERCIA Quercia Grossa about 1374 – Siena 1438

1 Study for the Fonte Gaia, Siena

Pen and brown ink, brown wash, on parchment. 7¹⁵⁄₁₆ × 8 ⅐₆in. (20.2 × 21.4 cm.)

Dick Fund, 49.141

In 1408 Jacopo della Quercia was commissioned by the city of Siena to execute a fountain ornamented with "sculptures, figures, foliage, cornices, steps, pilasters, and coats of arms" in the Piazza del Campo, opposite the Palazzo Pubblico. Work on the fountain, which was completed in 1419, did not begin until 1415; the municipal records show that an original project supplied in 1408 had been modified and enriched in 1409 and changed again in 1415. This fountain, traditionally called the Fonte Gaia, has been replaced in the Piazza del Campo by a weak modern replica, but fragments of the original are preserved in the Palazzo Pubblico in Siena. A fragmentary pen design on parchment in the Victoria and Albert Museum has been connected with the Fonte Gaia by Jeno Lányi (*Zeitschrift für Bildende Kunst,* 1926–1927, pp. 257–266), who suggested that the London drawing was part of the revised project supplied by Della Quercia in 1409. When the present drawing reappeared in 1949, it was immediately apparent that the vellum sheet had been the left section of a design of which the Victoria and Albert drawing represented the right section. Krautheimer, who published the Metropolitan's drawing shortly after its acquisition, pointed out that the middle section of the project, probably containing a central niche with a sculptured figure, is missing. He reaffirmed Lányi's suggestion that the design is related to the 1409 project. The fountain as executed differs in many respects from the drawings, though the freestanding figures on the projecting wings representing Acca Laurentia and Rhea Silvia, foster-mother and mother of Romulus and Remus, legendary founders of Siena, appear both in the drawings and on the fountain. It is Acca Laurentia and the infant twins who are represented at the left in our drawing. No other evidence of Della Quercia's style as a draughtsman has survived, and though the high quality of this and the London drawing speaks well for Jacopo's authorship, they may be the work of a studio assistant, acting on the sculptor's orders.

PROVENANCE: Erasmus Philipps; Richard Philipps, 1st Lord Milford (Lugt 2687); Sir John Philipps; purchased by the Metropolitan Museum in London in 1949.

BIBLIOGRAPHY: Richard Krautheimer, "A Drawing for the Fonte Gaia in Siena," *Metropolitan Museum of Art Bulletin,* June 1952, pp. 265–274, ill. p. 266.
John Pope-Hennessy, *Italian Gothic Sculpture,* London, 1955, p. 214 (our drawing described as probably a derivation from a design by Della Quercia).

PARRI SPINELLI Arezzo about 1387 – Arezzo 1453

2 La Navicella

Pen and brown ink. 10¹³⁄₁₆ × 15⅜ in. (27.5 × 39 cm.) Upper left and right corners of original sheet missing. Drawing pasted down on an old sheet that bears on its verso a Bandinellesque pen drawing after Masaccio's Adam and Eve Expelled from Paradise and a study of a seated male figure.

Inscription in pen and brown ink, probably in the artist's own hand, along side of boat: *la nave di giotto ch . . . i santo pietro a roma di musaicho;* in pen and brown ink in another hand at lower left: *Giotto*

Verso: Three pen sketches of ships that show through on recto.

Hewitt Fund, 19.76.2

Once considered to be Giotto's own design for the great mosaic representing Christ Walking on the Waters, in the entrance courtyard of the old basilica of St. Peter in Rome, this still very early drawing is instead a free copy after the mosaic by Parri Spinelli. Other drawn records of the mosaic in Parri's hand, reinterpreted each time with significant variants, are at Bayonne, Chantilly, and Cleveland (Berenson, 1961, nos. 1837 A, 1837 C, and 1837 K respectively). Degenhart has questioned Berenson's attribution of this group of drawings to Parri Spinelli, and given them to an anonymous Tuscan artist of the first half of the fifteenth century; however, the stylistic connection with drawings by Parri in the Uffizi and at Berlin is very convincing. Traditionally called La Navicella (the small ship), Giotto's mosaic still exists high above the entrance portico of the new St. Peter's, though ruined and then almost completely "modernized" in the seventeenth century. The Navicella was one of the great monuments of fourteenth century Rome, and it is not surprising that an artist visiting the city even a hundred years after its completion should be inspired by the celebrated composition.

PROVENANCE: Giorgio Vasari; Earls of Pembroke; Pembroke sale, London, Sotheby's, July 5–10, 1917, no. 515, ill., bought by the Metropolitan Museum.

BIBLIOGRAPHY: Strong, *Wilton House Drawings,* Part IV, no. 39.
Bryson Burroughs, "Drawings from the Pembroke Collection," *Metropolitan Museum of Art Bulletin,* June 1919, p. 136, ill. p. 138.
Adolfo Venturi, "La 'Navicella' di Giotto," *L'Arte,* XXV, 1922, p. 50, fig. 2.
Berenson, 1938, no. 1837 J, fig. 7.
Wilhelm Paeseler, "Giottos Navicella und ihr spätantikes Vorbild," *Römisches Jahrbuch für Kunstgeschichte,* V, 1941, pp. 49–162 (with previous bibliography on the mosaic), our drawing figs. 85, 93.
Metropolitan Museum, *European Drawings,* I, ill. no. 1.
Bernhard Degenhart, *Italienische Zeichnungen des frühen 15. Jahrhunderts,* Basel, 1949, pp. 26–27.
Claudia Refice, "Parri Spinelli nell'arte fiorentina dal sec. XV," *Commentari,* II, 3–4, 1951, p. 198, pl. LVII, fig. 239.
Claus Virch, "A Page from Vasari's Book of Drawings," *Metropolitan Museum of Art Bulletin,* March 1961, pp. 185–193, fig. 4 (recto), fig. 8 (verso).
Berenson, 1961, no. 1837 J, fig. 7.

EXHIBITIONS: Baltimore, Walters Art Gallery, 1962, The International Style. The Arts in Europe around 1400, no. 31, pl. XXXIV.

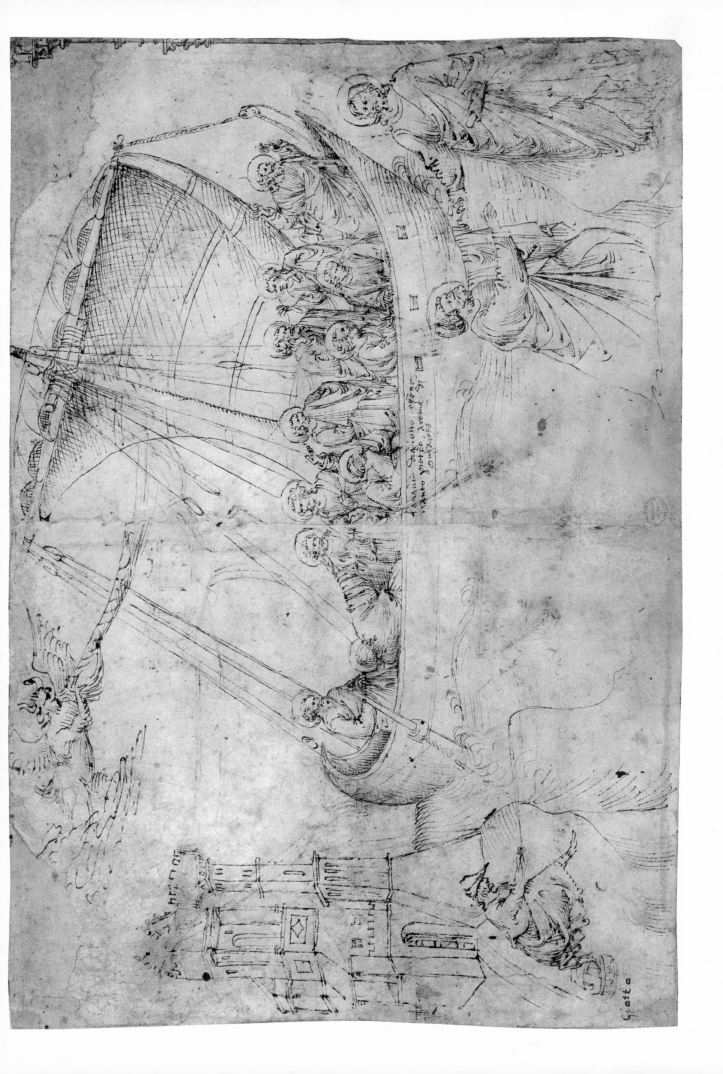

LEONARDO DA VINCI Vinci 1452 – Cloux 1519

3 Studies for a Nativity

Pen and brown ink, over preliminary sketches in metalpoint, on pink prepared paper. Ruled
   lines added in black chalk. 7⅝ × 6⁷⁄₁₆ in. (19.3 × 16.2 cm.)

Verso: Slight geometric sketches in pen and brown ink.   Rogers Fund, 17.142.1

In these four sketches of the Virgin, who kneels in humility before the Christ Child resting
on the ground, Leonardo investigated a theme that was to lead to the composition of the
Madonna of the Rocks, where the Virgin kneels facing the spectator, her right hand raised
in benediction over the seated infant Jesus. The sketch in the lower left corner, where the
Virgin raises both arms in devotional wonder, is close to a small composition study on a
sheet at Windsor Castle (ill. Popham, *Leonardo,* pl. 160). Both these sketches are related to a
design by Leonardo, which must have been brought at least to the stage of a complete
cartoon. Several old painted copies of this design have survived; the best known are in the
Uffizi (ill. Suida, *Leonardo,* fig. 48) and the Ashmolean Museum, Oxford. Recent controversy
over the chronology of the Paris and London versions of the Madonna of the Rocks makes
it difficult to date the Metropolitan drawing. If, as had generally been assumed, the Louvre
Madonna of the Rocks was the picture commissioned in Milan in 1483, then our drawing
may be dated at about that time. If, however, the National Gallery Madonna, a work finished
in Leonardo's late style, was the altarpiece originally commissioned in 1483, and the Louvre
picture was painted in Florence before the artist's departure for Milan, as Martin Davies
and Kenneth Clark contend, then our drawing might be appreciably earlier, and assignable
to Leonardo's first Florentine period.

PROVENANCE: J. G. Legrand; J. Allen Smith; Thomas Sully; Francis T. S. Darley; Thomas Nash; purchased
   by the Metropolitan Museum from Nash in New York in 1917.

BIBLIOGRAPHY: Bryson Burroughs, "Drawings by Leonardo da Vinci on Exhibition," *Metropolitan Museum of
   Art Bulletin,* October 1918, pp. 214–217, ill. p. 215.
   Popp, *Leonardo,* p. 37, pl. 19.
   Commissione Vinciana, II, no. 40.
   Suida, *Leonardo,* pp. 51, 270, pl. 49.
   Bodmer, *Leonardo,* ill. p. 149.
   Berenson, 1938, no. 1049 c, fig. 484.
   Metropolitan Museum, *European Drawings,* I, ill. no. 8.
   Popham, *Leonardo,* pp. 69, 149, pl. 159.
   Tietze, *European Master Drawings,* p. 42, no. 21, ill. p. 43.
   Clark, *Leonardo,* p. 42, pl. 20.
   Heydenreich, *Leonardo,* I, p. 183; II, pl. 34.
   Berenson, 1961, no. 1049 c, fig. 475.
   Charles de Tolnay, "Quelques dessins inédits de Léonard de Vinci," *Raccolta Vinciana,* fascicule
   XIX, 1962, pp. 110–111, fig. 13 (the hitherto unpublished verso of the sheet).

EXHIBITIONS: Philadelphia Museum of Art, 1950–1951, Masterpieces of Drawing, no. 21, ill.

LEONARDO DA VINCI Vinci 1452 – Cloux 1519

4 Head of a Man

Pen and brown ink, over traces of black chalk. 4⅝ × 2¹⁄₁₆ in. (11.6 × 5.2 cm.) Edges of sheet
torn irregularly.   Rogers Fund, 10.45.1

In this profile of an old man with sharply aquiline nose, down-slanted mouth, and knotted
brow, Leonardo has brought the "ideal" head almost to the limits of the grotesque. It is
not likely that this is a portrait or caricature; rather it is a conscious recollection of the ideal
portrait of Darius carved by Leonardo's master, Verrocchio. Verrocchio's bas-relief, sent
by Lorenzo the Magnificent to the king of Hungary, is now lost, but the profile is recorded
in a Della Robbia workshop terracotta relief in the Berlin Museum (ill. Leo Planiscig, *Andrea
del Verrocchio,* Vienna, n.d., pl. 38). A highly finished early drawing by Leonardo in the
British Museum (ill. Popham, *Leonardo,* pl. 129) must have been directly inspired by the
Verrocchio relief. Popham dates the British Museum drawing about 1480, and places our
sketch, where the powerful features of the imaginary Darius are recorded in a more forceful
and schematized fashion, about 1490. Leonardo's truly grotesque heads, exaggerated works
of pure fantasy, were, on the whole, done a good deal later in his career.

PROVENANCE: Sir Peter Lely (Lugt 2092); purchased by the Metropolitan Museum in London in 1909.

BIBLIOGRAPHY: *Vasari Society,* Part VII, 1911–1912, no. 2, ill.
Berenson, 1938, no. 1049 D.
Metropolitan Museum, *European Drawings,* I, ill. no. 10.
Popham, *Leonardo,* p. 64, p. 145, pl. 140 C.
Berenson, 1961, no. 1049 D, fig. 495.

LEONARDO DA VINCI Vinci 1452 – Cloux 1519

5 Allegory

Pen and brown ink. 7¹⁵⁄₁₆ × 5⅜ in. (20.2 × 13.3 cm.)

Inscription in pen and brown ink in the artist's hand, reading from right to left: *El ramarro fedele allomo vedēdo quello adormētato cōbatte cholla bisscia esse vede nōlla potere vincere core sopa, il volto dellomo ello dessta acchioche essa bisscia no noffenda lo adormentato homo.*

Verso: Pen studies for the Masque of Danae. Rogers Fund, 17.142.2

This mysterious allegorical representation of a man asleep, with his head resting perilously near the entangled group of a lizard struggling with a serpent, is open to as many interpretations as Leonardo's own reversed left-handed inscription will allow. Popham, who entitles the composition Allegory of the Lizard Symbolizing Truth, offers the following translation of the text: "The lizard faithful to man, seeing him asleep, fights with the serpent and, if it sees it cannot conquer it, runs over the face of the man and thus wakes him in order that the serpent may not harm the sleeping man." The circular form of the design suggests that it may have been intended for an allegorical emblem, probably done for the Sforza court in Milan. The drawing can be dated with some precision, for the verso of the sheet has presumably contemporaneous studies by Leonardo for the setting of the Masque of Danae, composed by Baldassare Taccone and represented on January 31, 1496 in the house of Giovanni Francesco Sanseverino, Conte di Cajazzo.

PROVENANCE: J. G. Legrand; J. Allen Smith (according to an inscription on the old mount that reads: *Souvenir d'amitié a J. allen Smith par J. G. Legrand en floréal an 9.*); Thomas Sully; Francis T. S. Darley; Thomas Nash; purchased by the Metropolitan Museum from Nash in New York in 1917.

BIBLIOGRAPHY: Bryson Burroughs, "Drawings by Leonardo da Vinci on Exhibition," *Metropolitan Museum of Art Bulletin,* October 1918, pp. 214–217.
Popp, *Leonardo,* p. 39, pl. 27.
Bodmer, *Leonardo,* ill. p. 233.
Commissione Vinciana, III, no. 106.
Berenson, 1938, no. 1049 B.
Metropolitan Museum, *European Drawings,* I, ill. no. 9.
Popham, *Leonardo,* pp. 59, 135, pl. III.
Heydenreich, *Leonardo,* I, p. 60; II, p. 64, pl. 81.
Berenson, 1961, no. 1049 B.

FILIPPINO LIPPI Prato 1457/58 – Florence 1504

6 Studies of Two Male Figures

Metalpoint, heightened with white gouache, on pink prepared paper. $9\frac{11}{16} \times 8\frac{1}{2}$ in. (24.6 × 21.6 cm.)

Verso: Metalpoint studies of hands, on pink prepared paper.   Dick Fund, 36.101.1

This study of two young models, one posed as St. Sebastian, the other seated with book in hand, is a typical and excellent example of an early Italian studio drawing. Although these two figures cannot be discovered in these particular poses in a painted work by Filippino Lippi, they must have been studied with a larger composition in mind. Filippino, like so many of his Florentine contemporaries, has used metalpoint on prepared paper to outline the figures and to indicate inner modeling; white gouache highlights give further plasticity to form. The drawing is one of a series of metalpoint studies of young models in Filippino's studio; other fine examples are in the Berlin and Dresden print rooms, the British Museum, the Uffizi, and the Pierpont Morgan Library. Our drawing has been attributed to Raffaellino del Garbo by Ulmann, and to Domenico Ghirlandaio by J. P. Heseltine, who once owned the sheet, but this very characteristic work by Filippino has from the first edition appeared under the artist's name in Berenson's work on Florentine drawings.

PROVENANCE: Lord de l'Isle; J. P. Heseltine; Henry Oppenheimer; Oppenheimer sale, London, Christie's, July 10–14, 1936, no. 112, ill., bought by the Metropolitan Museum.

BIBLIOGRAPHY: Hermann Ulmann, "Raffaellino del Garbo," *Reportorium für Kunstwissenschaft,* XVII, 1894, p. 113.
Hermann Ulmann, "Bilder und Zeichnungen der Brüder Pollajuoli," *Jahrbuch der Königlich Preussischen Kunstsammlungen,* XV, 1894, p. 244.
Berenson, 1903, no. 1349.
Original Drawings by Old Masters of the Italian School Forming Part of the Collection of J. P. H[eseltine], London, 1913, no. 22, ill.
A. E. Popham, *Italian Drawings Exhibited at the Royal Academy, Burlington House, London, 1930,* London, 1931, p. 14, no. 46, pl. XL.
Alfred Scharf, *Filippino Lippi,* Vienna, 1935, p. 124, no. 229, pl. 101, fig. 148.
Berenson, 1938, no. 1353 B.
Metropolitan Museum, *European Drawings,* I, ill. no. 5.
Tietze, *European Master Drawings,* p. 32, no. 16, ill. p. 33.
Mongan, *One Hundred Drawings,* p. 24, ill. p. 25.
Berenson, 1961, no. 1353 B.

EXHIBITIONS: London, Royal Academy of Arts, 1930, Exhibition of Italian Art, 1200–1900, no. 434.
Philadelphia Museum of Art, 1950–1951, Masterpieces of Drawing, no. 18, ill.

VITTORE CARPACCIO Venice 1460/65 – Venice about 1526

7 Study of a Youth in Armor

Point of brush and gray wash, heightened with white gouache, on blue paper. 7⁷⁄₁₆ × 7¹⁄₁₆ in.
(18.9 × 18 cm.)   The Elisha Whittelsey Collection, 54.119

This excellent example of a Renaissance studio drawing shows Carpaccio's young model dressed in a full suit of armor and posed as though he were on horseback, his arm raised with indication of a spear in his gloved hand. The artist may have intended to use this study in a composition representing the youthful St. George fighting the dragon, but the saint is quite differently represented in the series of canvases painted for the Scuola di San Giorgio degli Schiavoni about 1502–1508. Our drawing may be a rejected preparatory drawing for the St. George series, and Lauts dates it on stylistic grounds in the first decade of the sixteenth century. Typically Venetian is Carpaccio's use of the point of the brush, rather than metalpoint or pen and ink, to delineate form and to study the details of the suit of armor.

PROVENANCE: Purchased by the Metropolitan Museum in New York in 1954.

BIBLIOGRAPHY: Agnes Mongan, "Venetian Drawings in America," *Atti del XVIII Congresso Internazionale di Storia dell'Arte, 1955*, Venice, 1956, p. 304, fig. 201.
Giuseppe Fiocco, *Carpaccio,* Novara, 1958, pl. 100.
Jan Lauts, *Carpaccio, Paintings and Drawings,* London, 1962, pp. 273–274, no. 37, pl. 122.

EXHIBITIONS: London, P. & D. Colnaghi, 1954, Old Master Drawings, no. 12, ill.
Venice, Palazzo Ducale, 1963, Vittore Carpaccio, no. 14 in the catalogue of drawings, ill.

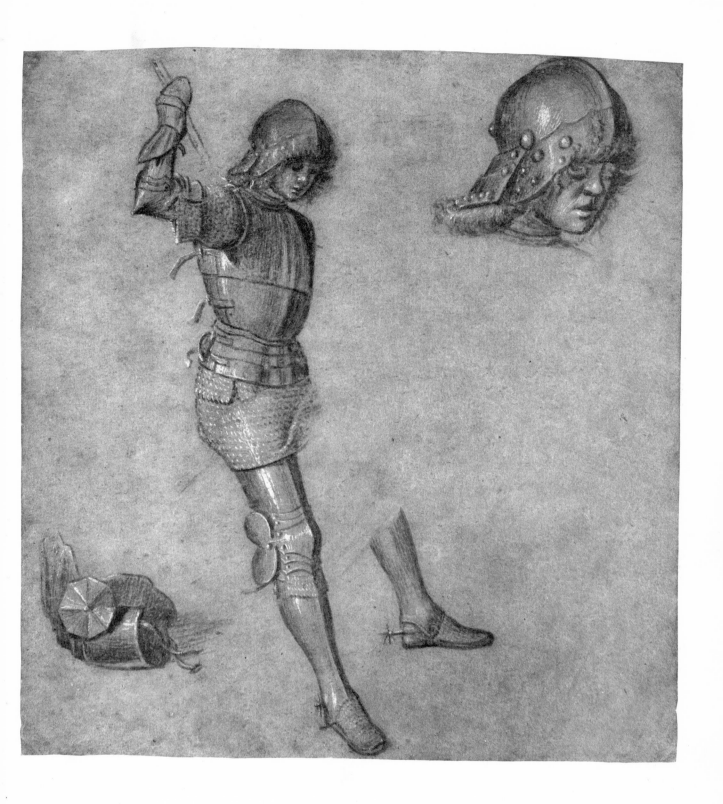

RAFFAELLINO DEL GARBO Florence about 1466 – Florence 1524

8 The Angel of the Annunciation

Pen and brown ink, brown wash, heightened with white gouache, on brown washed paper. Contours pricked for transfer. Diam. 3¾ in. (9.7 cm.)

Rogers Fund, 12.56.5a

Vasari reports that Raffaellino del Garbo, hard put to find commissions for large-scale panels, made many designs for ecclesiastical embroideries. The finish and the size of this roundel, with an elegant three-quarter-length figure of the angel of the Annunciation, go far to suggest that it may be a design for such an embroidery; the fact that the contours have been carefully pricked for transfer seems further evidence of the purpose of the design. A number of similar pricked and highly finished drawings by Raffaellino in the Uffizi and the British Museum have been generally accepted as embroidery patterns.

PROVENANCE: Sir Charles Eastlake, London; J. P. Richter, London; purchased by the Metropolitan Museum in London in 1912.

BIBLIOGRAPHY: Berenson, 1938, no. 766 A.
Metropolitan Museum, *European Drawings,* I, ill. no. 12.
Berenson, 1961, no. 766 E.

AMICO ASPERTINI Bologna 1475 – Bologna 1552

9 Bacchanalian Scene

Black chalk, heightened with white gouache, on brown washed paper. 10⅞ × 16¾ in. (27.6 × 42.6 cm.) Three diagonal creases at lower margin.   Rogers Fund, 08.227.27

This is a free and fanciful copy after Mantegna's engraving The Bacchanal with a Wine Press (Arthur M. Hind, *Early Italian Engraving,* London, 1948, Part II, V, p. 13, no. 4). Aspertini, *uomo capriccioso e di bizzarro cervello* according to Vasari, has transformed Mantegna's stately, measured composition into a curiously animated and rather sinister scene of alcoholic debauch. The artist traveled over all Italy, it is said, "copying every painting and relief, the good with the bad," but whatever he recorded seems to have been metamorphosed by the energy of his own strange, mad style. Three sketchbooks, one in a fragmentary state at Schloss Wolfegg, South Germany, and two in the British Museum, remain to testify to Aspertini's assiduity in recording motifs or compositions that interested him. The overwhelming majority of these drawings are free copies after antique sculpture, but one is not surprised to find that in the second British Museum sketchbook he has noted down two compositions by his ardently classicizing predecessor Mantegna (Phyllis Pray Bober, *Drawings after the Antique by Amico Aspertini,* London, 1957, pp. 81, 87, fig. 113). Our drawing may be contemporary with or perhaps a little later than these sketches, which Mrs. Bober dates about 1540.

In the Metropolitan's drawing, Aspertini's broad, brilliant use of white highlights to model heavy but rhythmic forms goes a long way to suggest the appearance of the now lost façade frescoes in grisaille for which he was celebrated in his time. This drawing came to the Museum in 1908 with an attribution to Lorenzo Leonbruno, a minor figure known for his imitations of Mantegna. Given the explicit derivation of the composition from Mantegna, the mistaken attribution is an understandable one. Philip Pouncey in 1958 was the first to point out that the drawing is an excellent and characteristic work of Aspertini.

PROVENANCE: Jonathan Richardson senior (Lugt 2184); purchased by the Metropolitan Museum in London in 1908.

BIBLIOGRAPHY: "Recent Acquisitions of Drawings," *Metropolitan Museum of Art Bulletin,* December 1908, p.224.

MICHELANGELO BUONARROTI Caprese 1475 – Rome 1564

10 Studies for the Libyan Sibyl

Red chalk. 11⅜ × 8⅜ in. (28.9 × 21.4 cm.) Spots of brown wash at lower right. Triangular section at right margin replaced.

Partially legible inscription in pen and light brown ink at lower left: *di M . . . nglo bonarroti.*; unidentified paraph in pen and darker brown ink at lower center.

Verso: Black chalk studies of legs and of a small seated figure. Inscriptions in pen and brown ink: at upper right, *58.*; at lower center, *n°. 21*

Purchase, Joseph Pulitzer Bequest, 24.197.2

This celebrated sheet bears a series of studies from a nude male model for the figure of the Libyan Sibyl that appears on the frescoed ceiling of the Sistine Chapel. The Sistine frescoes were commissioned in 1508 and finally unveiled in 1512. In the principal and highly finished drawing dominating the sheet Michelangelo has studied the turn of the sibyl's body, the position of the head and arms; in the fresco the sibyl turns to close a large book on a ledge behind her. The left hand of the figure is studied again below, as are the left foot and toes. A study of the sibyl's head, possibly the first drawing on the sheet, appears at the lower left, and a rough sketch of the torso and shoulders are immediately above it. A closely related drawing in the Ashmolean Museum at Oxford (Berenson, 1961, no. 1562, fig. 577) has red chalk studies for the sibyl's right hand and of the boy holding a scroll behind her. On the same sheet at Oxford occur studies for the slaves intended for the tomb of Julius II. The conjunction of studies for the Sistine ceiling and the tomb of Julius II gives evidence that the Libyan Sibyl, part of the very last phase of Michelangelo's work on the Sistine ceiling, was contemporary with the first plans for the ill-fated tomb. An old copy of our drawing with a few variants, possibly by a Northern artist, is in the Uffizi (ill. Paola Barocchi, *Michelangelo e la sua scuola. I Disegni di Casa Buonarroti e degli Uffizi*, Florence, 1962, no. 268, pl. CCLXIII).

PROVENANCE: Aureliano de Beruete, Madrid; purchased from Beruete's widow by the Metropolitan Museum in Madrid in 1924.

BIBLIOGRAPHY: Karl Frey, *Die Handzeichnungen Michelagniolos Buonarroti*, I, Berlin, 1909, pp. 2–4, pl. 4 (recto), pl. 5 (verso).
Bryson Burroughs, "Drawings by Michelangelo for the Libyan Sibyl," *Metropolitan Museum of Art Bulletin*, January 1925, pp. 6–14, ill. p. 8 (verso), p. 9 (recto).
A. E. Brinckmann, *Michelangelo. Zeichnungen*, Munich, 1925, p. 33, no. 32, pl. 32.
Berenson, 1938, no. 1544 D, fig. 631 (recto).
Metropolitan Museum, *European Drawings*, I, ill. no. 16 (recto), no. 17 (verso).
Tietze, *European Master Drawings*, p. 76, no. 38, ill. p. 77 (recto).
Mongan, *One Hundred Drawings*, p. 28, ill. p. 29 (recto).
Charles de Tolnay, *Michelangelo*, II, *The Sistine Ceiling*, Princeton, 1955, pp. 61, 204, no. 46, pl. 80 (recto); verso discussed p. 209, no. 13 A, pl. 236 (the author does not accept the verso as Michelangelo's work).
Parker, *Ashmolean Catalogue*, II, p. 141 (recto).
Luitpold Dussler, *Die Zeichnungen des Michelangelo*, Berlin, 1959, pp. 183–184, no. 339, pl. 39 (recto); verso discussed p. 183, no. 339, pl. 174 (the author does not accept the verso as Michelangelo's work).
Berenson, 1961, no. 1544 D, fig. 564 (recto), fig. 565 (verso).

EXHIBITIONS: Philadelphia Museum of Art, 1950–1951, Masterpieces of Drawing, no. 32, ill.

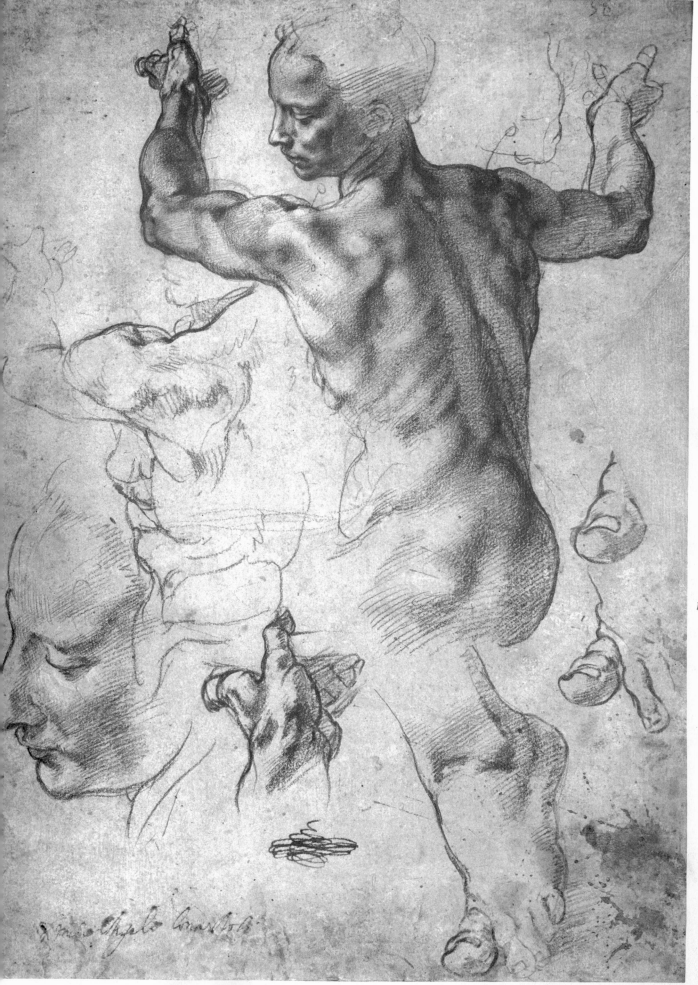

H

RAFFAELLO SANTI, called RAPHAEL Urbino 1483 – Rome 1520

11 Madonna and Child with the Infant St. John

Red chalk. 8¹³⁄₁₆ × 6¼ in. (22.4 × 15.4 cm.) Paper stained at lower right and at center; horizontal fold at center.

Inscription in pen and brown ink at lower left: *1509.* (?); in pen and brown ink at lower right: *Raf:...*

Rogers Fund, 64.47

This recently rediscovered drawing is a composition study for the Madonna im Grünen (Madonna in the Meadow), a picture in the Kunsthistorisches Museum in Vienna which bears a date that can be read as 1505 or 1506. Painted for Raphael's Florentine friend and patron Taddeo Taddei, the picture remained in the Palazzo Taddei in Florence until 1662, when it was purchased by the Archduke Ferdinand Karl and brought to Austria. Several of Raphael's preparatory drawings for the picture have survived. A double-faced sheet in the Albertina (Fischel, nos. 115, 116) bears pen sketches of alternative poses for the three figures, and the figure of the infant Baptist is represented both standing and kneeling. In a pen drawing in the Devonshire Collection at Chatsworth (Fischel, no. 117) the Baptist is studied standing and also kneeling to embrace the Christ Child. A drawing at the Ashmolean Museum in Oxford (Fischel, no. 118) executed with the point of a brush and pale brown wash comes close to the picture as executed, but the Metropolitan's drawing is the last in the sequence of preparatory drawings. It varies only in detail from the Vienna panel, and Crowe and Cavalcaselle, who must have seen the drawing, described it as a "small cartoon." There is, however, one significant variant between our drawing and the picture. The Madonna's right arm, free in the drawing, is covered in the painting with rather heavy drapery. In our design Raphael is concerned with establishing the general construction of the composition, where the three figures form a monumental triangle animated by the Leonardesque turn of the Virgin's torso and the arrested movement of the Christ Child, who reaches forward to seize the cross held by the infant Baptist. Only the staff of the cross, a prominent accent in the painting, is visible in our design. At the top of the sheet appear studies of the Virgin's drapery and the infant Baptist's right arm. The young Raphael has used red chalk with admirable ease to suggest the subtle contrasts of light and shade that model the figures; the drawing is one of the earliest examples of the artist's use of this drawing medium.

Engraved in reverse by Bernard Picart in 1734, when it belonged to the Dutch collector Antoine Rutgers, the Metropolitan Museum's drawing had previously belonged to Lambert ten Kate; from Rutgers it passed in turn to Ploos van Amstel, George Hibbert, and the poet Samuel Rogers. At the Rogers sale the sheet was purchased by T. Birchall, who lent it to the great Manchester Art Treasures exhibition in 1857. Then by inheritance it passed to the Rothwell family and the seclusion of an English country house, where it remained until its rediscovery in 1963. Modern scholars had assumed that the drawing was lost, and had known the design only through Picart's engraving of the recto of the sheet.

RAFFAELLO SANTI, called RAPHAEL   Urbino 1483 – Rome 1520

12   Nude Male Figure (verso of preceding drawing)

Pen and brown ink. 8¹³⁄₁₆ × 6¼ in. (22.4 × 15.4 cm.) Sheet considerably foxed at upper left.

Inscription in the artist's hand in pen and brown ink at lower right: *Carte de* . . . (the rest illegible); in pen and brown ink at lower left: *s. 89/4 66/4 H* . . .

Rogers Fund, 64.47

Raphael's pen study of a nude male figure is strikingly different in intention and treatment from the red chalk drawing for the Madonna in the Meadow on the recto of the same sheet. The figure has been drawn with a forceful pen line and sharp anatomical observation from a model in the studio, while the red chalk drawing, certainly not drawn from life, is a composition sketch where the artist is concerned with overall construction and lighting of a pictorial scheme and not with exact detail. The nude male figure, with head hanging limply forward and arms raised behind his back by cords that are hardly indicated, may well be a study for the figure of one of the thieves on the cross. Several drawings, datable on stylistic grounds to about the same time as the Metropolitan's sheet, testify that Raphael in his Florentine period had investigated solutions for a representation of the Descent from the Cross, and he may have intended to include the crucified thieves in the scene. On the verso of a sheet in the Albertina bearing a study for one of the predella panels for the 1507 Borghese Gallery Entombment of Christ is a pen design for a Descent from the Cross (Fischel, no. 182). Stylistically related to this Vienna sheet is a pen drawing in the Louvre (Fischel, no. 183) of a nude male figure hanging as from a cross; the figure is seen full length, but clearly derives from the male nude in our drawing. The somewhat dry and schematic draughtsmanship of the Paris sketch suggests that it is not a study from life, but one worked up from the example of the Metropolitan's drawing or a similar study after a model.

PROVENANCE: Lambert ten Kate Hermansz., Amsterdam; Ten Kate sale, Amsterdam, June 16, 1732, portfolio H, no. 31; Antoine Rutgers, Amsterdam; Rutgers sale, Amsterdam, December 1, 1778, no. 268; Cornelis Ploos van Amstel (Lugt 2034); Ploos van Amstel sale, Amsterdam, March 3, 1800, portfolio EEE, no. 3; George Hibbert, London; Hibbert sale, London, Christie's, June 12, 1833, no. 169; Samuel Rogers, London; Rogers sale, London, Christie's, beginning April 28, 1856, no. 951; T. Birchall; Richard Rainshaw Rothwell; J. W. Rothwell; sale, London Sotheby's, March 11, 1964, no. 150, bought by the Metropolitan Museum.

BIBLIOGRAPHY: Bernard Picart, *Impostures innocentes ou recueil d'estampes d'après divers peintres illustres, tel que Rafael, le Guide, Carlo Maratti, le Poussin, Rembrandt, etc.*, Amsterdam, 1734, pl. 5 (recto engraved in reverse).
J.-D. Passavant, *Raphaël d'Urbin et son père Giovanni Santi,* II, Paris, 1860, p. 496, no. 454.
Rudolf Weigel, *Die Werke der Maler in ihren Handzeichnungen,* Leipzig, 1865, p. 546, no. 6497.
J. A. Crowe and G. B. Cavalcaselle, *Raphael. His Life and Works,* I, London, 1882, p. 264.
Fischel, p. 140, note 2.
Parker, *Ashmolean Catalogue,* II, p. 267.
J. Bean, "A Rediscovered Drawing by Raphael," *Metropolitan Museum of Art Bulletin,* Summer 1964, pp. 1–10, ill. frontispiece (recto), p. 8, cover (verso).

EXHIBITIONS: Manchester, 1857, Art Treasures Exhibition, Drawings and Sketches of Old Masters, no. 49.

GIOVANNI ANTONIO DA PORDENONE
Pordenone 1484 – Ferrara 1539

13   St. Christopher

Pen and brown ink, brown wash, heightened with white gouache, on blue paper. Squared vertically and horizontally in black chalk, diagonally in red chalk. A number of spots of brown wash on the paper. 14¼ × 9¾ in. (36.2 × 24.8 cm.)

The Elisha Whittelsey Collection, 60.135

In 1528 Pordenone, an artist provincially trained in the Friuli, was commissioned to decorate the choir of the church of San Rocco in Venice. This work was to be his first and last major Venetian enterprise; Venice was not receptive to his strong and already highly personal style, and he was soon drawn to Emilia by more lucrative commissions. Little, unfortunately, remains of Pordenone's San Rocco frescoes, destroyed or repainted beyond recognition in the eighteenth century, but two panels with splendid figures of St. Christopher and St. Martin of Tours have survived (ill. Venturi, IX, 3, figs. 464, 465). Now hanging on the left wall of the church, these panels served originally as doors to a cupboard for ecclesiastical silver. Our drawing is an elaborate squared study for the figure of St. Christopher. The diagonal grid of squaring, superimposed on the more conventional vertical-horizontal pattern, reveals Pordenone's concern for the dramatic protobaroque diagonal stance of the giant figure; and the importance of the white gouache highlights in the modeling of the muscular figure announces the strong contrasts of light and shade in the panel. An old copy of our drawing, once in the collection of Baron Vivant-Denon and reproduced in his *Monuments des arts du dessin,* Paris, 1829, is now in the Crocker Gallery at Sacramento (Tietze, *Venetian Drawings,* no. A 1350). At Chantilly there is a red chalk study by Pordenone for the figure of St. Martin dividing his cloak in the pendant San Rocco panel (ill. Giuseppe Fiocco, *Giovanni Antonio Pordenone,* Udine, 1939, pl. 133).

PROVENANCE: John Skippe; the Martin family; Edward Holland Martin; Skippe sale, London, Christie's, November 20–21, 1958, no. 161; purchased by the Metropolitan Museum in London in 1960.

BIBLIOGRAPHY: Tietze, *Venetian Drawings,* p. 238, no. 1334, pl. XCIV, 4.
J. Bean, *Metropolitan Museum of Art Bulletin,* January 1962, ill. p. 161, fig. 4.

SEBASTIANO DEL PIOMBO Venice 1485 – Rome 1547

14 Seated Sibyl

Red chalk on beige paper. 9⅞ × 10⁷⁄₁₆ in. (24.4 × 26.5 cm.) All four corners replaced.
Inscription in pen and brown ink at upper left: *79*
Verso: study in pen and brown ink of a horse's head.

Gustavus A. Pfeiffer Fund, 62.120.7

This study of a seated sibyl listening to the whispered counsel of a ghostly genius who appears behind her was first identified as the work of Sebastiano del Piombo by Philip Pouncey. The drawing cannot be connected with any extant painted work by the artist, but it is not difficult to imagine this massive, hieratic figure watching over some sacred scene represented in a great fresco or panel painting. The heavy drapery, treated in broad sculptural folds, the powerful, noble profile of the sibyl, the curious foreshortening of her right shoulder, and the deliberate exaggeration of the size of her hands are all eminently typical of Sebastiano's mature style. The figure is certainly inspired by the sibyls in the Sistine Chapel, and the monumental sculptural style is also drawn directly from Michelangelo. Sebastiano's own Venetian pictorial tendencies are apparent in one of the most beautiful passages in the drawing, where the heavily accentuated profile of the sibyl is silhouetted against the shimmering suggestion of the head of the genius.

PROVENANCE: Hugh N. Squire, London; purchased by the Metropolitan Museum in London in 1962.
BIBLIOGRAPHY: J. Bean, *Metropolitan Museum of Art Bulletin,* March 1963, pp. 232–233, fig. 6.

TIZIANO VECELLIO, called TITIAN
Pieve di Cadore 1485/88 (?) – Venice 1576

15 A Group of Trees

Pen and brown ink on brownish paper. 8⁹⁄₁₆ × 12⁹⁄₁₆ in. (21.7 × 31.9 cm.)
Inscription in darker brown ink at lower margin: *Giorgione.*   Rogers Fund, 08.227.38

The old attribution to Giorgione inscribed on this splendid drawing is misleading, and since Colvin first published it in 1909 as the work of Titian it has generally been accepted as one of the rare examples of his landscape drawing. Von Hadeln hesitatingly placed the drawing in the circle of Titian, but the exceptional quality and power of the draughtsmanship testify convincingly in the favor of Titian's own authorship. The Tietzes have pointed out that the drawing was used in a woodcut after a design by Titian. In this print representing the Sacrifice of Abraham, the first version of which was executed by Ugo da Carpi, the trees in the left half of our drawing appear in reverse at the upper center, while the trees and the stump in the right half of the drawing appear in reverse near the lower right margin. What has not been observed before is that in the drawing itself the pen lines are somewhat blurred. This suggests that two ink counterproofs may have been made from the sheet in the course of transferring the outlines of the trees onto the large design that Titian must have supplied to the printmaker.

PROVENANCE: Charles Sackville Bale; Bale sale, London, Christie's, June 9, 1881, no. 2298 (as Giorgione); Sir James Knowles, London; Knowles sale, London, Christie's, May 27, 1908, no. 181 (as Titian), bought by the Metropolitan Museum.

BIBLIOGRAPHY: Sidney Colvin, *Vasari Society,* Part V, 1909–1910, no. 9, ill.
Detlev, Freiherr von Hadeln, *Titian's Drawings,* London, 1927, pp. 15–16, 24, pl. 45.
L. Frölich-Bum, "Die Landschaftszeichnungen Tizians," *Belvedere,* VIII, 1929, p. 77.
Hans Tietze and E. Tietze-Conrat, "Tizian-Studien," *Jahrbuch der Kunsthistorischen Sammlungen in Wien,* new series, X, 1936, pp. 167, 191, note 7, fig. 145 (related woodcut fig. 143).
Metropolitan Museum, *European Drawings,* I, ill. no. 14.
Tietze, *Venetian Drawings,* p. 321, no. 1943, pl. LXIII, 2.
Tietze, *European Master Drawings,* p. 54, no. 27, ill. p. 55.
Mongan, *One Hundred Drawings,* p. 48, ill. p. 49.
Hans Tietze, *Titian, the Paintings and Drawings,* London, 1950, p. 404, pl. 47.

EXHIBITIONS: Toledo Museum of Art, 1940, Four Centuries of Venetian Painting, no. 95.
Philadelphia Museum of Art, 1950–1951, Masterpieces of Drawing, no. 35, ill.
New York, Pierpont Morgan Library, 1953, Landscape Drawings and Water-Colors, no. 8.

ANTONIO ALLEGRI, called CORREGGIO
Correggio 1489/94 – Correggio 1534

17   Design for the Decoration of a Pilaster

Red chalk on beige paper. 12¾ × 8³⁄₁₆ in. (32.3 × 20.8 cm.)

Inscription in pen and brown ink in lower margin: *Correggio*.

Verso: Faint red chalk studies for the decoration of a pilaster with putto holding a quiver.

Hewitt Fund, 19.76.12

Building up from a tortoise placed on a double volute, the draughtsman has constructed a twisting column that works up through vase, cuirass, caduceus, helmet, and scabbard to a terminal cornucopia, supported along the way by putti, birds, and a satyr. Popham suggests that in spite of its entirely secular components, this lively ornamental construction may have been designed by Correggio for the painted decoration of the pilasters in the nave of San Giovanni Evangelista, Parma. The artist's overall commission for work in this church included the decoration of these pilasters, which were finally all ornamented with a standardized painted candelabrum. Attributed in an old inscription on the drawing itself to Correggio, and published as his by Strong, the drawing in recent years has been assigned to a number of artists, all influenced by Correggio. Venturi gave it to Bernardino Gatti, the Tietzes to Pordenone, Mrs. Heaton-Sessions to Pomponio Allegri. Popham has both prudently and convincingly returned it to Correggio himself, pointing out that it is entirely characteristic of the artist's draughtsmanship about the period of his activity in San Giovanni Evangelista.

PROVENANCE: Sir Peter Lely (Lugt 2092); Earls of Pembroke; Pembroke sale, London, Sotheby's, July 5–10, 1917, no. 409, bought by the Metropolitan Museum.

BIBLIOGRAPHY: Strong, *Wilton House Drawings,* Part V, ill. no. 47.
Adolfo Venturi, "Studii sul Correggio," *L'Arte,* V, 1902, pp. 353–354.
Sturge Moore, *Correggio,* p. 265.
Ricci, *Correggio,* p. 185.
Tietze, *Venetian Drawings,* no. 1360.
Heaton-Sessions, *Art Bulletin,* pp. 225–226, fig. 6.
Popham, *Correggio's Drawings,* pp. 62, 116, no. 47, pl. LIII.

Correggio

ANTONIO ALLEGRI, called CORREGGIO
Correggio 1489/94 – Correggio 1534

18 The Annunciation

Pen and black ink, gray wash, extensively heightened with white gouache, on red washed paper; squared off in red chalk. 3¾ × 6¹³⁄₁₆ in. (9.5 × 17.3 cm.)   Hewitt Fund, 19.76.9

In this small brush drawing Correggio suggests with almost magical ease and authority the pictorial effect of the fresco for which it is a study. The drawing, a miniature *modello,* must represent one of the last stages in the artist's preparation for the lunette painted for the church of the Annunziata at Capo di Ponte in Parma, now exhibited in a much damaged state in the gallery of that city (ill. Popham, *Correggio's Drawings,* pl. LVb). The fresco and the present drawing are dated about 1522–1524 by Popham, who compares them to Correggio's contemporary work in San Giovanni Evangelista in Parma. Several of the artist's preparatory drawings for this latter enterprise display the same vigorous and summary use of thick white gouache highlights to indicate modeling in light and shade.

PROVENANCE: Earls of Pembroke; Pembroke sale, London, Sotheby's, July 5–10, 1917, no. 465, bought by the Metropolitan Museum.

BIBLIOGRAPHY: Strong, *Wilton House Drawings,* Part III, ill. no. 25.
Sturge Moore, *Correggio,* pp. 121, 217, ill. opp. p. 242.
Bryson Burroughs, "Drawings from the Pembroke Collection," *Metropolitan Museum of Art Bulletin,* June 1919, p. 137, ill. p. 136.
Ricci, *Correggio,* p. 167, pl. CCLIIb.
Metropolitan Museum, *European Drawings,* I, ill. no. 19.
Heaton-Sessions, *Art Bulletin,* p. 224, fig. 1.
Popham, *Correggio's Drawings,* pp. 63, 159, no. 49, pl. LVa.

PIERO BUONACCORSI, called PERINO DEL VAGA

Florence 1501 – Rome 1547

19 The Presentation of the Virgin

Pen and brown ink, brown wash, heightened with white gouache, squared off in black chalk, on brownish paper. The empty triangular corners are tinted in gray-green wash, the right diagonal border tinted in gray wash. 8¹⁵⁄₁₆ × 10¹⁄₁₆ in. (22.7 × 25.5 cm.)

Rogers Fund, 63.75.1

It was probably early in the third decade of the sixteenth century that Perino del Vaga was commissioned by Cardinal Lorenzo Pucci to ornament the chapel in the left transept of the Trinità dei Monti in Rome. Perino's frescoes high up on the vault of this chapel have survived in a damaged state, but the rest of the work remained unfinished when the artist left Rome for Genoa in 1527, and the decoration was terminated a good deal later by Taddeo and Federico Zuccaro. On the four segments of the cross vault Perino painted scenes from the life of the Virgin. Preparatory drawings for three of these compositions—the Meeting at the Golden Gate, the Birth of the Virgin, and the Annunciation—have been identified in the Albertina and the Louvre (ill. Maria Vittoria Brugnoli, "Gli Affreschi di Perin del Vaga nella Cappella Pucci," *Bollettino d'Arte,* October–December 1962, figs. 9, 10, 11). The Metropolitan Museum's drawing for the fourth segment with the representation of the Presentation of the Virgin in the Temple has only recently reappeared. Like the Albertina drawing for the Meeting at the Golden Gate, it was once in the collection of Sir Thomas Lawrence. A red chalk drawing for the putti supporting Cardinal Pucci's arms at the summit of the entrance arch of the chapel is in the Ashmolean Museum at Oxford (ill. K. T. Parker, *Old Master Drawings,* XI, no. 43, December 1936, p. 42, pl. 38).

PROVENANCE: Prince Borghese, Rome (according to Lawrence Gallery catalogue); Sir Thomas Lawrence; Samuel Woodburn, London; Woodburn sale, London, Christie's, June 4–8, 1860, no. 981; sale, London, Sotheby's, March 12, 1963, no. 20, bought by the Metropolitan Museum.

BIBLIOGRAPHY: *The Lawrence Gallery, Fifth Exhibition. A Catalogue of One Hundred Original Drawings by J. Romano, F. Primaticcio, L. da Vinci, and Pierino del Vaga collected by Sir Thomas Lawrence,* London, 1835–1836, p. 30, no. 89.
Bernice Davidson, "Early Drawings by Perino del Vaga—I," *Master Drawings,* I, no. 3, Autumn 1963, p. 16, pl. 7a.

FRANCESCO MAZZOLA, called PARMIGIANINO
Parma 1503 – Casalmaggiore 1540

20   The Adoration of the Shepherds

Pen and brown ink, brown wash, heightened with white gouache, on brown washed paper.
8½ × 5¹⁵⁄₁₆ in. (21.6 × 14.1 cm.) Vertical and horizontal folds at center.

Rogers Fund, 46.80.3

Parmigianino arrived in Rome in 1524 and was active there until the sack of the city in 1527. From these years probably dates a group of free and spirited drawings in which he studied a number of alternative compositional schemes for an Adoration of the Shepherds where the Virgin is represented bathing the infant Christ. In addition to the present sheet, drawings in the Uffizi (747 E), the British Museum (1853-10-8-3 and 1856-6-14-2 verso), the École des Beaux-Arts in Paris (37143), and the Louvre (Inv. 6385) have been related by Mrs. Burroughs and by Popham to these compositional researches. Important and inventive variants distinguish these designs, though the seated cross-legged figure of St. Joseph pointing up at the flying angel in the Metropolitan Museum's drawing also occurs in the Louvre sketch. None of the drawings gives us the solution used by Parmigianino in the Adoration of the Shepherds, a picture datable in this Roman period, now in the Doria-Pamphilj Gallery (ill. Freedberg, *Parmigianino,* fig. 46). Our drawing was engraved in reverse by Metz in 1798. An old copy of the drawing is in the Horne Foundation (ill. Licia Ragghianti Collobi, *Disegni della Fondazione Horne in Firenze,* Florence, 1963, p. 24, no. 64, pl. 39, where it is wrongly attributed to Pellegrino Tibaldi).

PROVENANCE: Paignon-Dijonval; Vicomte Morel de Vindé, Paris; Sir Thomas Lawrence (Lugt 2445); William Coningham (Lugt 476); Dr. Frederic Haussmann, Berlin; purchased by the Metropolitan Museum in New York in 1946.

BIBLIOGRAPHY: C. M. Metz, *Imitations of Ancient and Modern Drawings . . . ,* London, 1798, ill. p. 72.

M. Bénard, *Cabinet de M. Paignon-Dijonval, état détaillé et raisonné des dessins et estampes dont il est composé,* Paris, 1810, p. 26, no. 391 (the folds in the sheet are mentioned).

The Lawrence Gallery, Fourth Exhibition, A Catalogue of One Hundred Original Drawings by Il Parmigianino and Ant. A. da Coreggio, London, 1835–1836, p. 9, no. 14.

Lili Fröhlich-Bum, *Parmigianino und der Manierismus,* Vienna, 1921, p. 95, ill. from Metz's facsimile, fig. 113.

Giovanni Copertini, *Il Parmigianino,* II, Parma, 1932, p. 60, ill. from Metz's facsimile, pl. CXLIIa.

Louise Burroughs, "A Drawing by Francesco Mazzola, Il Parmigianino," *Metropolitan Museum of Art Bulletin,* December 1948, pp. 101ff., ill. p. 102.

Freedberg, *Parmigianino,* p. 171, fig. 47.

FRANCESCO MAZZOLA, called PARMIGIANINO
Parma 1503 – Casalmaggiore 1540

21 Studies for the Figure of Moses

Pen and brown ink, brown wash, over slight traces of black chalk, on beige paper. 8¼ × 6¹⁄₁₆ in. (21 × 15.4 cm.)

Verso: Studies for the figure of Eve and architectural studies, in pen, brown ink, and wash.

Gustavus A. Pfeiffer Fund, 62.135

These nine sketches of the figure of Moses holding aloft the Tablets of the Law are studies for part of one of Parmigianino's major commissions, the decoration of the eastern apse and vaulting of the church of Santa Maria della Steccata in Parma. Other preparatory drawings—studies for individual figures and of the whole scheme—exist in the British Museum, the Louvre, Chatsworth, and elsewhere, and they reveal how elaborate were the artist's preparations for the project and how many alternative solutions came to his mind. Unfortunately, the artist was not as conscientious in his execution as in his preparation. He received the commission in 1531 with the understanding that the frescoes were to be completed within eighteen months. In 1535 the work was still unfinished, indeed hardly begun, and in 1539 Parmigianino was arrested on the order of his exasperated patrons. He escaped from Parma and died in exile the following year. The figures of Moses and the studies of Eve on the verso of the sheet are both related to the very small part of the decoration that was completed by Parmigianino himself. Moses and Eve appear painted in monochrome on the ribs of the vault of the eastern chapel of the church (ill. Freedberg, *Parmigianino*, figs. 99, 101).

PROVENANCE: Earl of Arundel; Antonio Maria Zanetti, Venice (according to the Lawrence Gallery catalogue); Baron Dominique Vivant-Denon (Lugt 779); Sir Thomas Lawrence (Lugt 2445); Captain Richard Ford; Ford sale, London, Sotheby's, April 25, 1934, no. 29; Sir Bruce Ingram; purchased by the Metropolitan Museum in London in 1962.

BIBLIOGRAPHY: Baron Dominique Vivant-Denon, *Monuments des arts du dessin,* II, Paris, 1829, pl. 157 (recto and verso in reverse).

The Lawrence Gallery, Fourth Exhibition, A Catalogue of One Hundred Original Drawings by Il Parmigianino and Ant. A. da Coreggio, London, 1835–1836, p. 10, no. 21.

A. E. Popham, *The Drawings of Parmigianino,* London, 1953, pp. 21, 40, 64, pls. LVI (recto), LVII (verso).

J. Bean, *Metropolitan Museum of Art Bulletin,* March 1963, pp. 231–232, figs. 3 (recto), 4 (verso).

EXHIBITIONS: Montreal Museum of Fine Arts, 1953, Five Centuries of Drawings, no. 46, ill.

Amsterdam, Rijksmuseum, 1955, Le Triomphe du maniérisme européen, no. 231.

London, Royal Academy of Arts, 1960, Italian Art and Britain, no. 468.

Rotterdam/Amsterdam, 1961–1962, 150 Tekeningen uit Vier Eeuwen uit de Verzameling van Sir Bruce en Lady Ingram, no. 142, pl. 2 (verso).

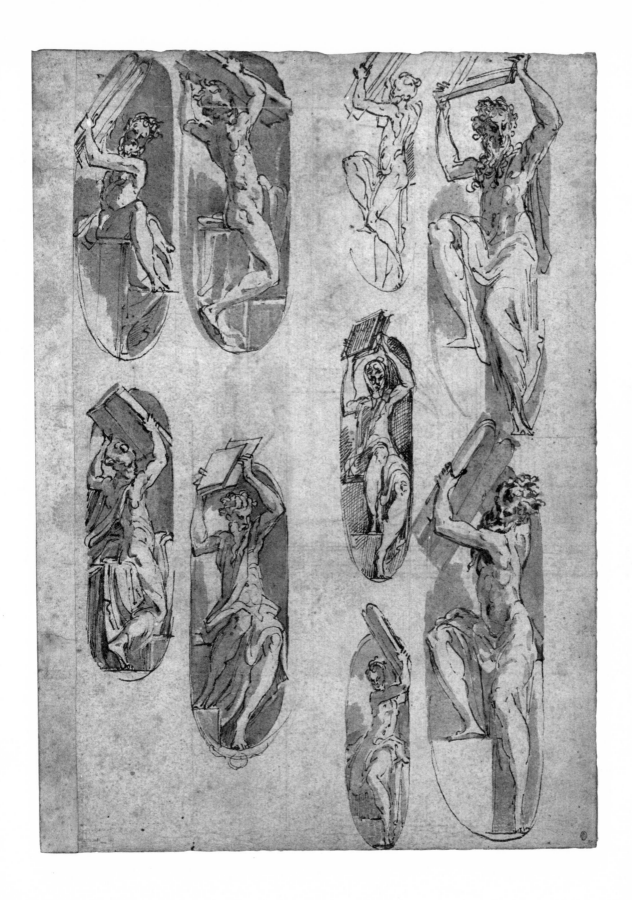

FRANCESCO PRIMATICCIO Bologna 1504 – Paris 1570

22 Vulcan Forging the Darts of Cupid

Red chalk, heightened with white gouache, on brownish paper. 13⅜ × 17³⁄₁₆ in. (34 × 43.7 cm.)
Sheet cut to the shape of a spandrel; vertical crease at center.   Hewitt Fund, 19.76.7

This is an elaborate preparatory drawing for one of the spandrels in the Salle de Bal at Fontainebleau. The painted decorations of this room, which survive in a disastrously reworked state, were executed between 1552 and 1556. Primaticcio supplied the designs for the frescoes, but the painting is said to have been largely the work of his talented assistant Niccolò dell'Abbate. The thick coat of nineteenth century repaint that veils the frescoes makes it difficult to discern the extent of Niccolò's participation; indeed, only Primaticcio's surviving drawings for the decoration enable us to conjure up the original richness and fantasy of the ornamentation on the somewhat awkward spaces that the architect of the room, Philibert de l'Orme, allowed the painter. The most conspicuous features of the scheme were the eight broad spandrels between the windows. In addition to the present drawing, five other designs for the spandrels survive: a further drawing in the Metropolitan Museum representing Discord at the Marriage Feast of Peleus and Thetis (no. 19.76.6, from the Wilton House Collection and acquired at the same time as the present drawing); a study for Apollo and the Muses on Mount Parnassus in the British Museum (1900-6-11-4); and drawings for the spandrels representing a Bacchanal and Ceres Presiding over the Harvest at Chantilly (ill. Louis Dimier, *Le Primatice,* Paris, 1928, pls. x, xi). Recently Dr. Fenyo has identified at Budapest a study for the spandrel representing Phaeton in Supplication before Apollo (Ivan Fenyo, "Dessins italiens inconnus du XVᵉ au XVIIIᵉ siècle," *Bulletin du Musée Hongrois des Beaux-Arts,* no. 22, 1963, pp. 97, 98, pl. 54).

PROVENANCE: Prosper Henry Lankrink (Lugt 2090); Earls of Pembroke; Pembroke sale, London, Sotheby's July 5–10, 1917, no. 500, bought by the Metropolitan Museum.

BIBLIOGRAPHY: Strong, *Wilton House Drawings,* Part V, ill. no. 52.
Metropolitan Museum, *European Drawings,* I, ill. no. 25.

EXHIBITIONS: New London, Connecticut, Lyman Allyn Museum, Fourth Anniversary Exhibition, 1936, no. 48, ill.
Cambridge, Fogg Art Museum, Anxiety and Elegance, the Human Figure in Italian Art 1520–1580, 1962, no. 28.

PAOLO FARINATO Verona 1524 – Verona 1606

23 Allegorical Female Figure Holding Tablet and Crown

Brush and brown wash over black chalk. 15 13/16 × 11 1/8 in. (40.1 × 28.3 cm.)

Long inscription in pen and brown ink in the artist's hand at lower left. Inscription in pen and brown ink in another hand at lower center: *P. Farinat.*   Rogers Fund, 62.119.9

Farinato must have drawn this seated female figure as a project for the decoration of a spandrel, the triangular space formed by the outer curve of an arch and its enclosing moldings. His inspiration was sculpture—such spandrel figures in bas-relief play an important role in Venetian architectural decorations—and the drawing may be a study for an exterior fresco in imitation of sculpture. A rapid broad brush drawing over a slight chalk sketch creates contrasts of light and shade that emphasize the easy decorative curve of the ornamental figure, rather than particularizing the rather synthetic structure of the body. The artist has used the empty lower left corner of the sheet to note down a recipe for pills against the plague.

PROVENANCE: William Roscoe, Liverpool (according to inscription on verso of mount); Studley Martin, Liverpool; Martin sale, Liverpool, January 29, 1889, no. 396 (according to inscription on verso of mount); O'Byrne Collection; sale, London, Christie's, May 1, 1962, no. 70, ill., bought by the Metropolitan Museum.

BIBLIOGRAPHY: J. Bean, *Metropolitan Museum of Art Bulletin,* March 1963, p. 235, fig. 7.

p far pilore cotra l...
p̄ste pihandone ogni · s̄ ...
la matina · 2 ore ināti mang...

Pilia prima ū quarto mira
     ū quarto zafra
    dūi quarti aloe epreso insieme
    inpoluere E poi pilia s̄... aceto̅
di cedro p̄ inpastar dite̅ poluere
et far lepilore pihandone una
al sopra scrito modo
Receta de m̄ ʒuane copino

P. Firmat

FEDERICO BAROCCI Urbino 1526 – Urbino 1612

24 Studies of Heads and Hands

Black chalk, heightened with white and a little red chalk, on blue paper. 11 × 16¼ in. (28 × 41.3 cm.) Lower right corner replaced.   Rogers Fund, 50.143

These heads and hands are studies for the figure of the apostle seated third from the right of Christ in a large version of the Last Supper, painted by Barocci for the Chapel of the Blessed Sacrament in the Duomo at Urbino (ill. Venturi, IX, 7, p. 944, fig. 529). This late work of the artist, dating from 1592–1599, was paid for by contributions from Francesco Maria II della Rovere, duke of Urbino. Olsen lists more than fifty drawings for the Last Supper, and these testify to the care with which Barocci prepared his canvases and to his mastery of bold, broad modeling in black and white chalk.

PROVENANCE: The Earls Spencer (Lugt 1530); Spencer sale, London, June 10, 1811, no. 22; Lionel Lucas (Lugt 1733a); Lucas sale, London, Christie's, December 9, 1949, no. 54; purchased by the Metropolitan Museum in London in 1950.

BIBLIOGRAPHY: Marilyn Aronberg Lavin, "A Late Work by Barocci," *Metropolitan Museum of Art Bulletin,* May 1955, pp. 267–268, ill. p. 271.
Harald Olsen, *Federico Barocci, A Critical Study in Italian Cinquecento Painting* ("Figura," no. 6), Stockholm, 1955, p. 158.
Harald Olsen, *Federico Barocci,* Copenhagen, 1962, pp. 82, 203, pl. 92a.

FEDERICO ZUCCARO Sant'Angelo in Vado about 1542 – Ancona 1609

26 The Vision of St. Eustace

Point of brush, brown, gray, green, yellow, and red wash, heightened with white gouache, over traces of black chalk; lightly squared off in black chalk. $13\frac{7}{16} \times 7\frac{15}{16}$ in. (34.1 × 20.2 cm.)

Rogers Fund, 62.76

This water-color drawing is the finished squared study for a fresco executed on the façade of a small palace on the Piazza Sant'Eustachio in Rome about 1560, when Federico Zuccaro was eighteen. Vasari recounts that this was Federico's first important commission, obtained for him by his elder and already successful brother Taddeo. The work in progress, presumably visible to all who passed through the square, caused so much favorable comment that Taddeo grew jealous and reworked part of the fresco, so that the best of the execution would be said to be his. Federico, enraged, destroyed his brother's additions. Through the intervention of friends peace was made between the brothers, and once Federico had finished the fresco it was hailed as a triumph for the young artist. The relevant passage from Vasari was transcribed on the back of the old mount by the Richardsons, who once owned the drawing. The fresco decoration survives in a damaged and repainted state. It differed from monochrome Roman wall frescoes of the earlier sixteenth century in that it was executed in a variety of colors, already present in our drawing. The treatment of the trees and rocks, indicated broadly with the point of a brush and colored washes, is most original in Italian draughtsmanship, and looks forward, as Gere has pointed out, to the celebrated tree studies of Barocci in the Louvre, the British Museum, and the Lugt Collection. It should be recalled that Barocci came into contact with the Zuccaro brothers in Rome at just about the time of the Sant'Eustachio frescoes.

PROVENANCE: Jonathan Richardson senior (Lugt 2184); Jonathan Richardson junior (Lugt 2170); Sir Joshua Reynolds (Lugt 2364); purchased by the Metropolitan Museum in London in 1962.

BIBLIOGRAPHY: J. Bean, *Metropolitan Museum of Art Bulletin,* March 1963, p. 232, fig. 5.
J. A. Gere, "Two Panel-pictures by Taddeo Zuccaro—II," *Burlington Magazine,* CV, no. 726, September 1963, p. 394, note 12.

ANNIBALE CARRACCI Bologna 1560 – Rome 1609

27 Anteros Victorious

Red chalk. 8¾ × 6¼ in. (22.2 × 15.9 cm.)
Inscription in pen and brown ink at lower left: *annibale Caracci*.

Gustavus A. Pfeiffer Fund, 62.120.2

Annibale Carracci's major Roman enterprise was the frescoed decoration of the vault of the
Gallery of the Palazzo Farnese, begun in 1597 and finished about 1604. This decoration was
conceived as a complex but completely logical interweaving of full-scale, independent
painted compositions in simulated frames (*quadri riportati*) and illusionistic architectural
painting (*quadratura*). At the four corners of the cove vault of the long gallery the painted
architecture opens to reveal triangular glimpses of painted sky, against which are silhouetted
pairs of putti standing on balustrades. These putti are combined to represent contrasts between spiritual and sensuous loves; the theme of the decoration of the Gallery is the Loves
of the Gods. In one corner Cupid and Anteros are represented struggling for the palm
branch, and a black chalk drawing in the Louvre (Inv. 7305; exhibited at Bologna, 1956,
Mostra dei Carracci, Disegni, no. 188) is Annibale's study for this solution. The Metropolitan Museum's drawing represents an earlier stage of the artist's planning for this
corner, a stage at which the artist thought of representing the victorious Anteros holding
aloft the disputed palm branch and being carried by two putti. Popham has pointed out
that the group studied in our drawing is probably based on a composition of three putti
lifting up a fourth, engraved as an invention of Parmigianino and also recorded in two
pictures attributed to Parmigianino in English collections, one at Knole, the other at
Brocklesby Park. Preparatory studies by Annibale for the putti in the other three corners
of the Farnese ceiling fresco are at Windsor Castle, the Louvre, Besançon, and in the Ellesmere Collection.

PROVENANCE: Lionel Lucas (Lugt 1733a); Lucas sale, Christie's, London, December 9, 1949, part of no. 67;
Hugh N. Squire, London; purchased by the Metropolitan Museum in London in 1962.

BIBLIOGRAPHY: Michael Jaffé, "The Carracci at Newcastle," *Burlington Magazine,* CIV, January 1962, p. 26,
fig. 29.
J. Bean, *Metropolitan Museum of Art Bulletin,* March 1963, p. 231, ill. cover.

EXHIBITIONS: London, P. & D. Colnaghi, 1950, Old Master Drawings, no. 10.
Newcastle upon Tyne, King's College, 1961, The Carracci, Drawings and Paintings, no. 136,
pl. XXXVI.

annibale Carraci

ANNIBALE CARRACCI Bologna 1560 – Rome 1609

28 Study of an Angel

Black chalk, heightened with white chalk, on blue paper. 14 × 9¾ in. (35.5 × 24.6 cm.) Two
    spots of rose-colored paint at lower left.
Inscription in pen and black ink at lower right corner: *8.*
Verso: Black chalk study of a cushion.   Gustavus A. Pfeiffer Fund, 62.120.1

In the very first years of the seventeenth century Cardinal Antonio Maria Salviati commissioned from Annibale Carracci an altarpiece to ornament a chapel in the church of San
Gregorio Magno in Rome. The subject chosen was St. Gregory Praying for the Souls in
Purgatory; the saint was represented kneeling, facing the spectator and attended by two
youthful angels, one on his knees to the left of the saint, the other standing at the right.
Probably begun before the cardinal's death in April 1602, the picture was no doubt finished
when the chapel was consecrated in October 1603. From Rome the St. Gregory altarpiece,
a majestic work of Annibale's mature Roman style, found its way into the Ellesmere Collection at Bridgewater House in London, where unfortunately it was burned during World
War II. Our drawing, a study from a young model in the studio, with angel wings indicated
above his shoulders, was made in preparation for the angel on the right. Annibale has ex-
perimented with a number of alternative positions for the angel's right arm and hand, but
the final position of the arm in the drawing corresponds quite closely to that detail in the
picture. On the verso of the sheet is a study for the cushion on which St. Gregory kneels.
Only two other drawings for the St. Gregory altarpiece seem to have survived: an elaborate
compostition study with many variants at Chatsworth (ill. *Old Master Drawings from Chatsworth,* Washington, D.C., New York, etc., 1962–1963, pl. 13) and a freer composition study
at Windsor Castle (Rudolf Wittkower, *The Drawings of the Carracci at Windsor Castle,* London,
1952, p. 145, no. 351).

PROVENANCE: Hugh N. Squire, London; purchased by the Metropolitan Museum in London in 1962.
BIBLIOGRAPHY: Michael Jaffé, "The Carracci at Newcastle," *Burlington Magazine,* CIV, January 1962, p. 26,
             fig. 28.
             J. Bean, *Metropolitan Museum of Art Bulletin,* March 1963, pp. 225–227, 231, ill. frontispiece.
EXHIBITIONS: Newcastle upon Tyne, King's College, 1961, The Carracci, Drawings and Paintings, no. 154,
             pl. XLI.

8

FRANCESCO VANNI Siena 1563 – Siena 1610

29 The Virgin with St. Catherine and St. Bernardino of Siena

Pen and brown ink, brown wash, over black chalk, on brownish paper. 8¾₁₆ × 10¾ in. (20.8 × 27.3 cm.)

Inscription in pen and brown ink at lower right: *Vanni*; at lower left: *2*.

Gustavus A. Pfeiffer Fund, 62.120.8

In this spirited composition sketch, Vanni offers us a synthesis of Sienese imagery. The Virgin, patroness of the city and the preferred subject of Sienese painting from the thirteenth through the sixteenth centuries, appears surrounded by angels and putti and adored by St. Bernardino and St. Catherine, protectors of the city. Below is indicated the skyline of Siena, easily identified by the silhouettes of the Torre del Mangia and of the cupola and campanile of the Duomo. The limits of the composition, which cannot be related to a surviving picture, are indicated by lines above and to the right; further to the right the artist has sketched ornamental motifs supporting heraldic animals.

PROVENANCE: Padre Sebastiano Resta, Milan; Monsignor Giovanni Matteo Marchetti, bishop of Arezzo; Cavaliere Marchetti of Pistoia; John, Lord Somers (Lugt 2981); Richard Houlditch (Lugt 2214); Jonathan Richardson senior (Lugt 2183, 2995, 2996, 2983, 2984, 2992, 2992a); Sir Joshua Reynolds (Lugt 2364); Hugh N. Squire, London; purchased by the Metropolitan Museum in London in 1962.

GIOVANNI FRANCESCO BARBIERI, called GUERCINO
Cento 1591 – Bologna 1666

30 Youth Kneeling before a Prelate

Pen and brown ink, brown wash. 9⅜₁₆ × 7½ in. (23.7 × 19.1 cm.)

Verso: Another study of a youth before a prelate in pen and brown ink, brown wash, partially visible on recto.   Rogers Fund, 08.227.29

This is a dashing free sketch of the principal figures in an altarpiece representing St. William, duke of Aquitaine, receiving the monastic habit, painted in 1620 for the church of San Gregorio in Bologna and now in the Pinacoteca of the same city (ill. Ellis Waterhouse, *Italian Baroque Painting,* London, 1962, fig. 96). Guercino's preparations for this large picture, justly celebrated as one of his most sumptuous early works, are recorded in preparatory drawings at the Louvre and at Windsor Castle. In the picture St. William, kneeling before St. Benedict of Aniane who is seated at the left, pulls a monastic cowl over his head; a Windsor drawing (Inv. 2475) gives us this solution. In three drawings at the Louvre (Inv. 6884, 6885, 6886) St. William, kneeling or standing before the prelate, already wears the habit. On both the recto and verso of the Metropolitan sheet the kneeling saint, still clad in armor, holds a cross in his hand, and this scheme is elaborated in reverse with the addition of other figures in a further Louvre drawing (Inv. 6883; ill. Gabriel Rouchès, *Musée du Louvre. Dessins italiens du XVIIᵉ siècle,* Paris, n.d., no. 14). A complete composition study with notable variants was in the collection of Baron Vivant-Denon (ill. *Monuments des arts du dessin,* III, Paris, 1829, pl. 209).

PROVENANCE: William Russell (Lugt 2648); purchased by the Metropolitan Museum in London in 1908.

BIBLIOGRAPHY: Roger Fry, "Recent Acquisitions of Drawings," *Metropolitan Museum of Art Bulletin,* January 1909, p. 7.

GIOVANNI FRANCESCO BARBIERI, called GUERCINO
Cento 1591 – Bologna 1666

31 Standing Boy Holding a Bowl

Red chalk. 10⅞₁₆ × 7⅞₁₆ in. (26.5 × 18.9 cm.)   Rogers Fund, 63.75.2

This red chalk drawing of a boy in scant classical drapery holding a bowl to his lips may be a study for a figure of Ganymede, cupbearer of the gods. Neither a Ganymede nor this particular youthful figure is to be found in any of Guercino's surviving pictures, but the style of this sensitive drawing, where subtle contrasts of light and shade so successfully indicate the modeling of the back and head, suggests that it probably dates from the artist's middle period. In any case, the red chalk is used more freely than in the smoothly finished figure drawings produced in such abundance by Guercino in his later years.

PROVENANCE: Edward Bouverie (Lugt 325); John, Lord Northwick; Northwick sale, London, Sotheby's, November 4, 1920, no. 14; sale, London, Sotheby's, March 12, 1963, no. 34, ill., bought by the Metropolitan Museum.

PIETRO BERRETTINI, called PIETRO DA CORTONA
Cortona 1596 – Rome 1669

32   The Triumph of Nature over Art

Pen and brown ink, brown wash, over black chalk. 7⅞ × 5¹³⁄₁₆ in. (20 × 14.7 cm.)

Rogers Fund, 61.2.1

Pietro da Cortona made this design as one of the illustrations for a treatise on gardening by a learned Jesuit, Giovanni Battista Ferrari. This volume, *De Florum Cultura*, appeared in Rome in 1633 with Cortona's design engraved in reverse by Johann Friedrich Greuter; an Italian translation of the work, in which the same illustration was used, appeared in 1638. The artist illustrates an allegorical passage in Ferrari's text that tells of a contest between Nature and Art. Art, kneeling at the right with grafting knife in hand, has produced a rose bush with blossoms of three colors, but Flora at the right is about to crown Nature, who stands pointing at the miracle of her own doing. As if by magic a Chinese rose tree has sprung from the ground, and while Vertumnus dances holding a sistrum aloft, three boys, Lucifer, Meriggio, and Hesper, identified respectively by a lily branch, a rose, and a bleeding heart, and representing Dawn, Noon, and Evening, circle the tree while its flowers change from white, to pink, to scarlet, as they are said to do in the course of a day. The wonders of Nature are seen to be more marvelous than those of Art. A drawing by Cortona for another illustration in Ferrari's book is in the Prado at Madrid (ill. Anthony Blunt and Hereward Lester Cooke, *The Roman Drawings of the XVII and XVIII Centuries . . . at Windsor Castle,* London, 1960, p. 76, fig. 57).

PROVENANCE: Dr. Alfred Ritter von Wurzbach-Tannenberg (Lugt 2587); Anton Schmid (Lugt 2330b); sale, Munich, May 17–18, 1956, no. 30; purchased by the Metropolitan Museum in New York in 1961.

BIBLIOGRAPHY: J. Bean, *Metropolitan Museum of Art Bulletin,* January 1962, ill. p. 162, fig. 5.

PIETRO BERRETTINI, called PIETRO DA CORTONA
Cortona 1596 – Rome 1669

33   A Wind God

Black chalk, heightened with white chalk, on brownish paper. 7⅞₆ × 13⅛ in. (18.9 × 33.3 cm.)
The irregular edge of sheet has been filled in at all sides.

The Elisha Whittelsey Collection, 61.129.1

This youthful figure is a study for a wind god who appears on the frescoed ceiling of the Sala di Apollo in the Palazzo Pitti, Florence. Pietro da Cortona undertook the decoration of the state rooms along the façade of the Pitti in 1641. The Sala di Giove was the first to be executed, then the Sala di Marte. Work on the Sala di Apollo seems hardly to have begun when Cortona left for Rome in 1647, and Ciro Ferri, his Florentine assistant, using Cortona's designs, finished the fresco as late as 1660. Vitzthum has remarked that the advanced style of this drawing suggests that it may have been made by Cortona in Rome and sent to Ferri in Florence to guide him in his work. He has further pointed out that a sheet by Cortona in the Gabinetto Nazionale delle Stampe in the Farnesina at Rome (F.C. 124327 verso) bears a study for a section of the Sala di Apollo ceiling in which the wind god is clearly visible. Drawings by Cortona for other sections and figures in the frescoes in this room are in the Uffizi, the Louvre, and the Farnesina in Rome.

PROVENANCE: George Hibbert (Lugt 2849); Nathaniel Hibbert; Sir Henry Thurston Holland, 1st Viscount Knutsford and his heirs; sale, London, Sotheby's, April 11, 1935, no. 78; L. G. Duke, London; purchased by the Metropolitan Museum in London in 1961.

BIBLIOGRAPHY: J. Bean, *Metropolitan Museum of Art Bulletin,* January 1962, ill. p. 159, fig. 2.
Giuliano Briganti, *Pietro da Cortona,* Florence, 1962, p. 307, pl. 287, no. 53 (the fresco pls. 231–234).
Walter Vitzthum, in a review of Briganti's monograph, *Master Drawings,* I, no. 2, Summer 1963, p. 50.

EXHIBITIONS: Leicester Museum and Art Gallery, 1952, Old Master Drawings, no. 26.
London, Royal Academy, 1953, Drawings by Old Masters, no. 151.

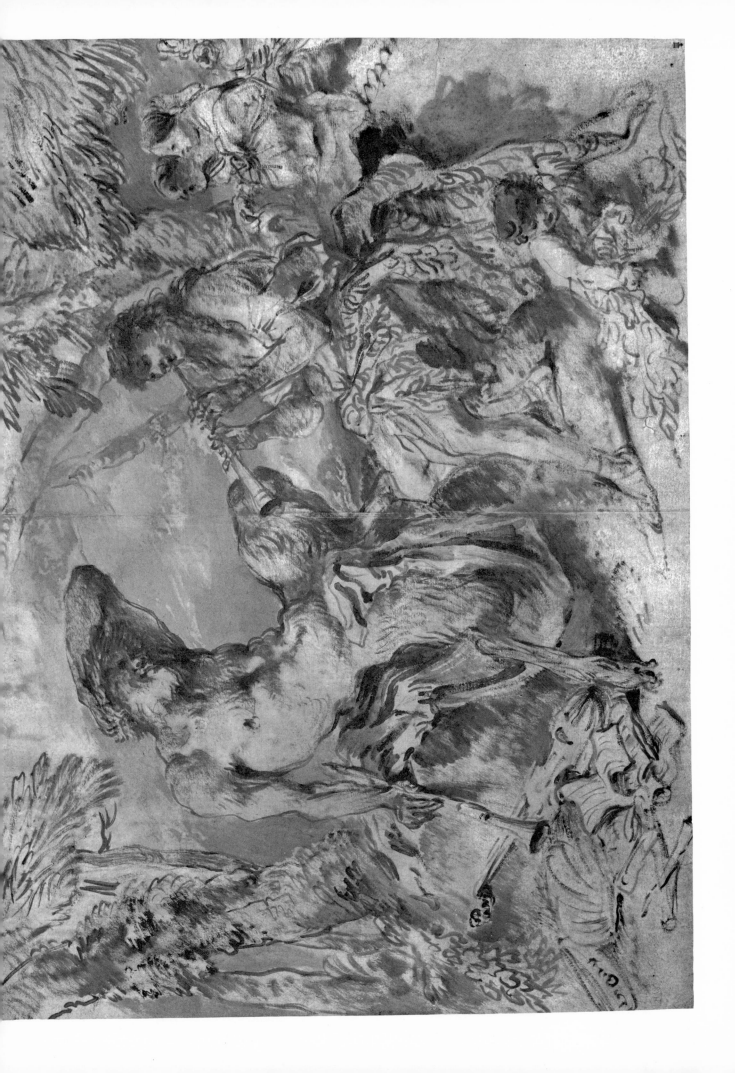

STEFANO DELLA BELLA Florence 1610 – Florence 1664

35 Design for a Monstrance

Pen and brown ink, gray wash, over black chalk. 15⅜ × 9½ in. (39.1 × 24.1 cm.)

Rogers Fund, 61.131.1

Stefano della Bella, whose talent was essentially that of a decorator, made a number of sketches for ornamental metalwork. This design for a monstrance is unusually large and complete. At Windsor there is a less finished pen study for a similar monstrance, supported by three angels with upraised arms (Anthony Blunt, *The Drawings of G. B. Castiglione and Stefano della Bella . . . at Windsor Castle,* London, 1954, p. 95, no. 44); the Uffizi possesses a series of smaller designs for oil lamps, and there were many ornament drawings in an album of Della Bella's sketches formerly in the collection of Sir George Holford, sold at Sotheby's, May 22, 1928, no. 29B.

PROVENANCE: The Earls Spencer (Lugt 1530); Spencer sale, London, June 10, 1811, no. 236 or no. 237; Dr. Barry Delany (Lugt 350); purchased by the Metropolitan Museum in London in 1961.

SALVATOR ROSA Naples 1615 – Rome 1673

36 Witches' Sabbath

Pen and brown ink, brown and a little gray wash. 10¹¹⁄₁₆ × 7¼ in. (27.2 × 18.4 cm.)

Rogers Fund, 12.56.13

Sometimes said to represent the Temptation of St. Anthony, this drawing, a particularly brilliant example of Rosa in his most inventive mood, evokes instead a fantastic scene of incantation. Witches armed with cabalistic symbols conjure from the fire a ghostly skeleton and a fire-breathing dragon that appear above. In overall composition and in many important details the drawing is related to a picture in the Corsini Collection in Florence, which must date from the 1640s. The historian Baldinucci records this commission: "Al marchese Bartolommeo Corsini dipinse un bel quadro d'incantesimi e stregonerie"—a fine picture of incantations and witchcraft (Filippo Baldinucci, *La Vita di Salvatore Rosa,* Venetian edition of 1830, p.56). Another version of the Corsini picture was once in the Stroganoff Collection, and a further replica is in a private collection in Rome. A sheet in the Uffizi (12,102 F) bears rapid pen sketches related to figures in our drawing and in the Corsini picture.

PROVENANCE: Sir Charles Greville (Lugt 549); George Guy, 4th Earl of Warwick (Lugt 2600); J. P. Richter, London; purchased by the Metropolitan Museum in London in 1912.

BIBLIOGRAPHY: Tietze, *European Master Drawings,* p. 160, no. 80, ill. p. 161.
Walter Vitzthum, "Le Dessin baroque à Naples," *L'Oeil*, no. 97, January 1963, ill. p. 50.
Luigi Salerno, *Salvator Rosa,* Rome, 1963, p. 63.

CARLO MARATTI Camerano 1625 – Rome 1713

37 Study for an Altarpiece

Pen and brown ink, red chalk, and a little red wash. 17¹³⁄₁₆ × 10¼ in. (45.3 × 25.8 cm.)
Arched top torn irregularly; slight repairs in brush and gray wash in another hand at
top of arch.

Inscription in pen and brown ink at lower left: *C° Maratti.*   Rogers Fund, 63.18

Maratti's altarpiece for the important Cybo chapel in the Roman church of Santa Maria del
Popolo represents St. John the Evangelist, St. Gregory, St. John Chrysostum, and St.
Augustine anachronistically grouped together in a discussion of the doctrine of the Im-
maculate Conception, which is represented symbolically above them. This picture, a splendid example of Maratti's mature style, was commissioned by Cardinal Alderano Cybo and
finished in 1686. An unusually complete series of preparatory drawings for the altarpiece
has survived, and in the alternative compositional solutions that Maratti investigated we
can observe the caution and the high seriousness of the artist's working methods. In addition to the present drawing, composition studies with important variants are at Düsseldorf,
Windsor Castle, Chatsworth, the Uffizi, the Pierpont Morgan Library in New York; and
the Metropolitan Museum possesses another freer sketch for the altarpiece. The drawings
at Düsseldorf and in the Morgan Library are closest to the picture. Studies for individual
figures in the altarpiece are in the British Museum, the Berlin print room, and at Düsseldorf.

PROVENANCE: William Mayor (Lugt 2799); C. R. Rudolf (Lugt 2811b); purchased by the Metropolitan Museum
in London in 1963.

BIBLIOGRAPHY: K. T. Parker, "Carlo Maratti," *Old Master Drawings,* X, no. 39, December 1935, p. 46, pl. 45.
Amalia Mezzetti, "Contribuiti a Carlo Maratti," *Rivista dell'Istituto Nazionale d'Archeologia e
Storia dell'Arte,* new series, IV, 1955, p. 337.
Francis Dowley, "Some Maratti Drawings at Düsseldorf," *Art Quarterly,* XX, Summer 1957,
pp. 171–174.

EXHIBITIONS: Leicester Museum and Art Gallery, 1952, Old Master Drawings, no. 40.
London, Arts Council, 1962, Old Master Drawings from the Collection of Mr. C. R. Rudolf,
no. 36.

LUCA GIORDANO Naples 1632 – Naples 1705

38 The Triumph of Cybele

Brown wash over black chalk. 14¾ × 21 in. (37.5 × 53.3 cm.) Vertical crease just left of center; missing passage replaced at center of lower margin.

Inscription in brush and gray wash at right margin: *Jorda* . . . ; in pen and brown ink at lower margin: *N°. 72, 324 pˢ, 4 . . . 28.*　　　　　　　　Rogers Fund, 63.76.4

This brilliant example of late baroque draughtsmanship has all the characteristics of Giordano's work during his ten-year stay in Spain, one of the most productive but least known periods of his astonishing career. Walter Vitzthum has recently pointed out that this figure of the earth goddess Cybele, crowned with city towers, holding a key in her hand, and riding triumphantly in a chariot drawn by lionesses, is a preparatory study for a section of the ceiling fresco in the principal room of the Casón del Buen Retiro in Madrid. The relevant detail of the fresco, which represents the story of the Order of the Golden Fleece, is reproduced by Yves Bottineau, "À Propos du séjour espagnol de Luca Giordano," *Gazette des Beaux-Arts*, LVI, November 1960, p. 253. The Uffizi possesses a somewhat smaller study for the group of Minerva in full battle regalia and her warlike attendants, seen opposite Cybele in the Buen Retiro ceiling (Uffizi no. 6698 F).

PROVENANCE:　　Sale, London, Sotheby's, February 27, 1963, no. 21 (as anonymous Italian, seventeenth century), bought by the Metropolitan Museum.

SEBASTIANO RICCI Belluno 1659 – Venice 1734

39 Figure Studies

Pen and brown ink, blue-gray wash, over red and a little black chalk. 11⅛ × 7½ in.
(28.3 × 19 cm.) Gustavus A. Pfeiffer Fund, 62.120.6

The figures on this sheet of studies by Ricci are grouped with so much grace and art that one might think that the artist is preparing a specific religious or historical composition. Actually, he seems to have been engaged in a superior form of artistic doodling. Other sheets of studies by Ricci in the Louvre (Inv. 14,271) and the British Museum (1960-4-9-114) have similar elegant figures jotted in the same fashion on the page, and none is related to a known picture. In drawing such sketches Ricci kept himself in practice, and when called upon to compose one of his vast pictures, his memory and his sketchbooks could supply him with a whole repertory of graceful poses and groups. Ricci is a Janus-like figure in Venetian art. At once conservative and progressive, he looks back to Paolo Veronese (and indeed this sheet recalls Veronese's own sketches) and forward to Giovanni Battista Tiepolo, on whom he had a decisive influence.

PROVENANCE: John Barnard (Lugt 1419 and 1420); Hugh N. Squire, London; purchased by the Metropolitan Museum in London in 1962.

BIBLIOGRAPHY: J. Bean, *Metropolitan Museum of Art Bulletin,* March 1963, p. 235, fig. 8.

GIOVANNI BATTISTA TIEPOLO Venice 1696 – Madrid 1770

41 The Adoration of the Magi

Pen and brown ink, brown wash, over a little black chalk. 16⁷⁄₁₆ × 11⁷⁄₁₆ in. (41.7 × 29 cm.)
Rogers Fund, 37.165.16

This dramatically conceived Adoration of the Magi is still a relatively early design by
G. B. Tiepolo. Benesch dated the drawing in the 1730s, and called attention to its connection with another early drawing of the same subject with notable variants, in the Cleveland
Museum of Art (ill. H. S. Francis, " 'The Adoration of the Magi,' a Drawing by Giovanni
Battista Tiepolo," *Bulletin of The Cleveland Museum of Art*, January 1946, p. 1). Much later,
in 1753, Giovanni Battista painted a further variant version of the Adoration of the Magi in
a large altarpiece now in the Alte Pinakothek in Munich; an even later and quite different
composition is studied in an oil sketch in the Metropolitan Museum (ill. Morassi, 1955, pl.
50 and fig. 40 respectively).

PROVENANCE: Edward Cheney (?); Marquis de Biron, Paris and Geneva; purchased by the Metropolitan
Museum in Geneva in 1937.

BIBLIOGRAPHY: Benesch, *Venetian Drawings*, p. 30, pl. 15.

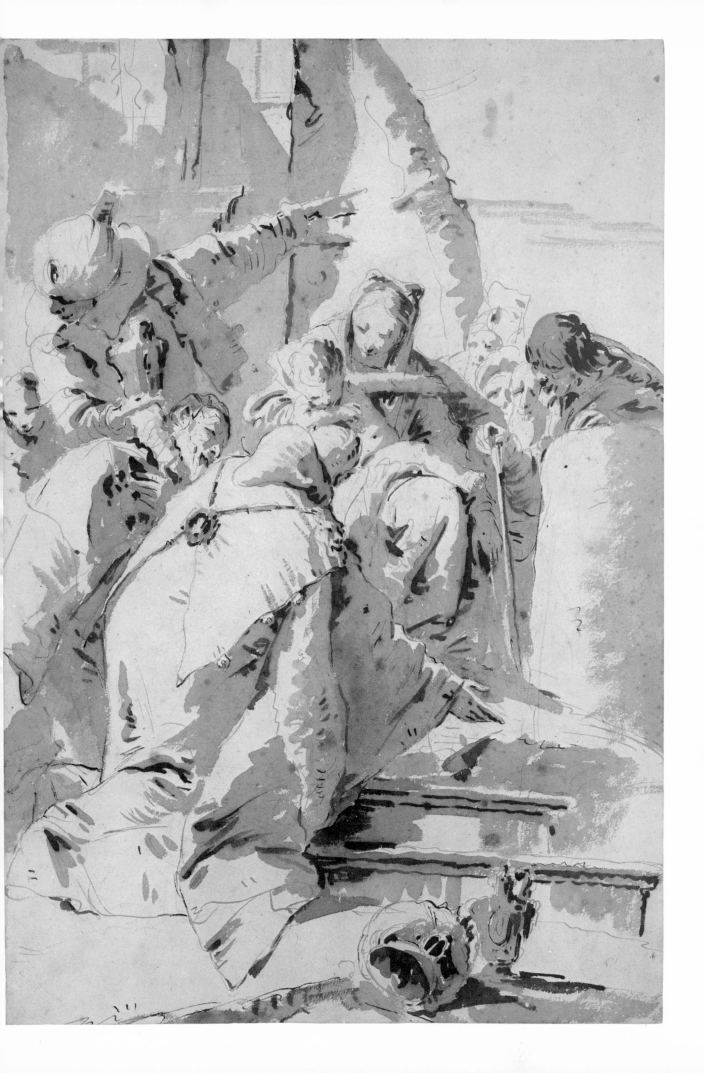

GIOVANNI BATTISTA TIEPOLO Venice 1696 – Madrid 1770

42 River God and Nymph

Pen and brown ink, brown wash, over a little black chalk. 9¼ × 12⅝ in. (23.5 × 31.3 cm.)
Rogers Fund, 37.165.32

This river god and his attendant nymph appear reclining on the edge of a painted cornice at one end of the ceiling Giovanni Battista Tiepolo painted in fresco in the Palazzo Clerici at Milan in 1740 (ill. Morassi, 1955, pl. 26), and stylistically the drawing is closely related to a long series of brilliant studies for the Palazzo Clerici ceiling. These "Clerici" drawings, which probably belonged to the English collector Edward Cheney, are now for the most part in the Metropolitan Museum, the Pierpont Morgan Library in New York, and the Horne Foundation in Florence. Some twelve years later Tiepolo used the same nymph and river god on the edge of the frescoed ceiling of the Kaisersaal of the Würzburg Residenz (ill. Morassi, 1955, pl. 56). It is possible that our Palazzo Clerici study may have been used as the model for the repetition of the group at Würzburg. Only in his early years did Tiepolo produce drawings for sale; the drawings of his maturity seem to have been kept in his studio, where they served as a repertory of compositional motifs.

PROVENANCE: Edward Cheney (?); Marquis de Biron, Paris and Geneva; purchased by the Metropolitan Museum in Geneva in 1937.

BIBLIOGRAPHY: Metropolitan Museum, *European Drawings,* I, ill. no. 41.
Max H. von Freeden and Carl Lamb, *Das Meisterwerk des Giovanni Battista Tiepolo, Die Fresken der Würzburger Residenz,* Munich, 1956, pl. 44.

EXHIBITION: Chicago, Art Institute, 1938, Loan Exhibition of Paintings, Drawings, and Prints by the Two Tiepolos, no. 70, ill.
New York, Metropolitan Museum of Art, 1938, Tiepolo and His Contemporaries, no. 45, ill.

GIOVANNI BATTISTA TIEPOLO Venice 1696 – Madrid 1770

43 The Meeting of Anthony and Cleopatra

Pen and brown ink, brown wash, over a little black chalk. 16⅟₁₆ × 11½ in. (40.8 × 29.2 cm.)
Rogers Fund, 37.165.10

The Meeting of Anthony and Cleopatra, in a magnificent setting of illusionistic architecture by Mengozzi-Colonna, is the subject of one of Tiepolo's frescoes in the Salone of the Palazzo Labia in Venice, painted in the 1740s. The poses of the two principal figures in our drawing differ considerably from the Palazzo Labia fresco, but the drawing must date from about this time. Indeed, the two figures grouped as they are in the drawing occur in an oil sketch for a quite differently composed Meeting of Anthony and Cleopatra, now in the collection of Baron Philippe de Rothschild in Paris (ill. Morassi, 1955, fig. 30). This oil sketch is a study for a large canvas by Giovanni Battista, dated 1747, at Arkhangelskoye, the former country house of the Jusupov family near Moscow, where the figures of Anthony and Cleopatra are arranged in yet another fashion (ill. Morassi, 1962, fig. 313). The complicated inner relationship between the Palazzo Labia fresco, the oil sketch in Paris, the painting at Arkhangelskoye, and our drawing is typical of the complex chronology of Giovanni Battista Tiepolo's vast and unfailingly inventive production.

PROVENANCE: Edward Cheney (?); Marquis de Biron, Paris and Geneva; purchased by the Metropolitan Museum in Geneva in 1937.

BIBLIOGRAPHY: Metropolitan Museum, *European Drawings,* I, ill. no. 38.

ANTONIO CANAL, called CANALETTO
Venice 1697 – Venice 1768

45   Man Smoking a Pipe

Pen and brown ink, over black chalk. 11⅝ × 6⁷⁄₁₆ in. (29.6 × 16.3 cm.)
Inscriptions in the same ink as the drawing at upper right of both recto and verso: *40/volta.*
Verso: pen study of a standing gentleman and two studies of his head.

Purchase, Joseph Pulitzer Bequest, 39.79

Very few preparatory drawings for the figures that stroll through Canaletto's Venetian *vedute* have survived, and the male figures sketched on the recto and verso of this sheet are not immediately identifiable in any extant picture. However, a very similar drawing at the Courtauld Institute in London, numbered in the same fashion as our drawing and possibly from the same dismembered sketchbook, bears a figure that occurs in a view of San Giacomo di Rialto, datable about 1746, now in the National Gallery of Canada at Ottawa (ill. Constable, *Canaletto,* no. 839 for the Courtauld drawing, no. 298 for the Ottawa picture). Like the London drawing, our study is drawn in Canaletto's most supple and meandering pen line.

PROVENANCE: Purchased by the Metropolitan Museum in New York in 1939.

BIBLIOGRAPHY: Metropolitan Museum, *European Drawings,* I, ill. no. 35.
K. T. Parker, *The Drawings of Canaletto in the Collection of His Majesty the King at Windsor Castle,* Oxford and London, 1948, p. 26, note 37.
Constable, *Canaletto,* I, pl. 159 (recto and verso); II, p. 565, no. 840.

40
notta.

FRANCESCO GUARDI Venice 1712 – Venice 1793

46 The Villa Loredan, near Treviso

Pen and brown ink, brown wash, over black chalk. 15¾ × 30 in. (40 × 76.1 cm.) Vertical crease at center.   Rogers Fund, 37.165.69

This large view of the gate and the façade of a Venetian villa was used by Guardi in a picture of approximately the same dimensions, now in a private collection in London (ill. Antonio Morassi, *Arte Veneta*, no. 4, 1950, p. 53, fig. 49). In the picture figures have been added, and they stand outside the villa and on the road in the foreground. A fairly exact copy after the picture, drawn by Francesco himself or by his son Giacomo, is in the Ashmolean Museum at Oxford. This copy bears an inscription that identifies the now destroyed villa: *View of the Seat of S. E. Loredano at Paese near Treviso at present in the possession of John Strange Esqr. N. B. grass ground within the Fence; without the post road from Treviso to Bassan.* John Strange was British Resident in Venice from 1773 to 1790 and a patron of the then little known Francesco Guardi. The artist made several drawings at the Villa Loredan. A smaller freer sketch of the entrance gate and façade is at the Rhode Island School of Design in Providence (ill. *Master Drawings Selected from the Museums and Private Collections in America*, Buffalo, Albright Art Gallery, 1935, pl. 73). A view from the front windows of the villa is at the Fodor Museum in Amsterdam, and a view from the back windows in the Ashmolean Museum. The painted view of the façade corresponding to our drawing is one of a series of four pictures formerly in Lord Rothermere's collection. The other pictures represent the garden façade of the Villa Loredan, the façade and garden of the neighboring Villa dal "Timpano Arcuato," and the gardens of the Palazzo Contarini dal Zaffo in Venice. There are drawings for these last two pictures at Rotterdam, Oxford, and Lille (Winslow Ames has recently published the Lille drawing in *Master Drawings*, I, no. 3, Autumn 1963). Byam Shaw has suggested that Guardi's drawings of the Villa Loredan probably date from 1778, when the painter undertook a journey from Venice to his family home in the Val di Sole.

PROVENANCE: Marquis de Biron, Paris and Geneva; purchased by the Metropolitan Museum in Geneva in 1937.

BIBLIOGRAPHY: Byam Shaw, *Guardi,* p. 65, no. 30, pl. 30.
Parker, *Ashmolean Catalogue,* II, pp. 509–511 (the copy after the painted view of the façade of the villa is pl. CCXIX).
K. T. Parker, *Disegni Veneti di Oxford,* Venice, 1958, pp. 73–75.
K. T. Parker and J. Byam Shaw, *Canaletto e Guardi. Catalogo della Mostra dei Disegni,* Venice, 1962, pp. 76–77.

EXHIBITIONS: New York, Pierpont Morgan Library, 1953, Landscape Drawings and Water-Colors, no. 20.

FRANCESCO GUARDI Venice 1712 – Venice 1793

47 Figure Studies

Pen and brown ink, brown wash, on blue paper. Faint black chalk sketch of a figure at
  lower left. 6⅜ × 8⅝ in. (16.2 × 21.8 cm.)
Signed in pen and brown ink at lower left: *f.co Guardi.*

Gift of Harold K. Hochschild, 40.91.3

Francesco Guardi was in the habit of making rapid abbreviated sketches of accessory figures
—*macchiette,* as they are called in Italian—which he used over and over again to animate his
painted views, whether realistic or imaginary. Byam Shaw has pointed out that the lady
and gentleman at the lower right and the family group above both appear in a view of the
Piazzetta with a crowd of senators, formerly in the Gutekunst Collection (ill. *Pantheon,* I,
1928, opp. p. 87). The lady with her high feathered headdress (a feature that dates the sheet
in the last dozen years of the painter's activity) and her escort also appear in a picture at
Bergamo and in another at the National Gallery in London. We encounter them again in
another drawing at the Metropolitan Museum, a sketch for an architectural *capriccio* (37.
165.81; ill. Max Goering, *Francesco Guardi,* Vienna, 1944, pl. 113) and in a drawing at the
Victoria and Albert Museum (ill. Byam Shaw, *Guardi,* pl. 60). The present drawing is signed
by the artist himself in characteristic fashion; a similar signature appears on another sheet
of *macchiette* in the Metropolitan Museum (40.91.2; ill. Byam Shaw, *Guardi,* pl. 50).

PROVENANCE: Richard Ederheimer, New York; Harold K. Hochschild, New York.
BIBLIOGRAPHY: Byam Shaw, *Guardi,* p. 72, no. 51, pl. 51.

Fco Guardi.

FRANCESCO GUARDI Venice 1712 – Venice 1793

48 The Stairway of the Giants

Pen and brown ink, brown wash, over red chalk. 10⅜ × 7⁵⁄₁₆ in. (26.3 × 18.5 cm.)
Rogers Fund, 37.165.85

Though this rapid and brilliant pen sketch has all the air of an architectural *capriccio,* it is a fairly accurate view—by Guardi's standards—of the Scala dei Giganti in the courtyard of the Palazzo Ducale in Venice. The principal architectural features of the staircase and of the arcaded courtyard have been recorded by the draughtsman, but Jacopo Sansovino's giant statues of Mars and Neptune at the top of the stairs have been transformed into twisting draped figures in a rococo taste. The cloaked figures ascending the staircase, jotted down in the most abbreviated fashion, add an even more decisive "contemporary" note to the scene. The style of the drawing suggests that it is a fairly late work by Guardi. A drawing of the Scala d'Oro in the Palazzo Ducale, again with variants to suit the taste of the draughtsman, is in the Museo Correr in Venice (ill. Byam Shaw, *Guardi,* pl. 58), and the Metropolitan Museum has another drawing of figures on a staircase that seems to be entirely a creation of the artist's fantasy (37.165.72).

PROVENANCE: Marquis de Biron, Paris and Geneva; purchased by the Metropolitan Museum in Geneva in 1937.

BIBLIOGRAPHY: Benesch, *Venetian Drawings,* p. 39, no. 59, pl. 59.

GIOVANNI DOMENICO TIEPOLO Venice 1727 – Venice 1804

49 A Caricatured Figure and Studies of Heads

Pen and brown ink, brown wash, over a little black chalk. 10⅝ × 7⁵⁄₁₆ in. (27.1 × 18.5 cm.)
Signed in pen and brown ink at lower right: *Domᵒ Tiepolo f.*   Rogers Fund, 37.165.68

The style of this caricature of a gentleman with a cane, signed by Domenico Tiepolo, testifies to the son's dependence on his father, Giovanni Battista, and to his mastery of this aspect of his father's draughtsmanship. The character heads sketched at the top of the sheet occur in a series of etchings by Domenico; the bearded Oriental at the upper right recalls Rembrandtesque types introduced to Venice through the drawings and etchings of Giovanni Benedetto Castiglione.

PROVENANCE: Marquis de Biron, Paris and Geneva; purchased by the Metropolitan Museum in Geneva in 1937.

BIBLIOGRAPHY: Metropolitan Museum, *European Drawings,* I, ill. no. 60.
J. Byam Shaw, *The Drawings of Domenico Tiepolo,* London, 1962, p. 90, no. 78, pl. 78.

EXHIBITIONS: Chicago, Art Institute, 1938, Loan Exhibition of Paintings, Drawings, and Prints by the Two Tiepolos, no. 114.
New York, Metropolitan Museum of Art, 1938, Tiepolo and His Contemporaries, no. 74, ill.

GINO SEVERINI born Cortona 1883

50 Still Life

Charcoal and pieces of the front page of *La Presse* of September 3, 1914. 22⅛ × 18⅝ in.
(56.2 × 47.3 cm.)   The Alfred Stieglitz Collection, 49.70.20

Severini signed the original Manifesto of Futurist Painting in 1910 and showed with the
futurists in their first Paris exhibition of 1912. The superimposed and rather agitated cylin-
drical forms at the top of this drawing, which dates from 1914, have an unmistakably
futurist air, but here they are constrained to play a constructive role in a composition of
the strictest cubist obedience. *Papier collé* is used with considerable authority to give greater
relief to the drawn passages of the design. Picasso and Braque, whom Severini knew and
obviously admired, had used pieces of pasted paper to reinforce the plasticity of their cubist
constructions. However, Severini himself, by sticking sequins onto the canvas of his
Dynamic Hieroglyphic of the Bal Tabarin (now in the Museum of Modern Art, New York)
in the summer of 1912, may have anticipated true cubist collages by several months, as
Alfred Barr has pointed out. Severini had a one-man show at Alfred Stieglitz's New York
gallery in 1917; this drawing figured in the exhibition and in 1949 came to the Metropolitan
Museum in the Stieglitz Bequest with four other important drawings of the artist's most
creative period.

PROVENANCE: Alfred Stieglitz, New York.

EXHIBITIONS: New York, "291" (Alfred Stieglitz's gallery), 1917.
                New York, An American Place, 1937, Beginnings and Landmarks: "291" 1905–1917, no. 67.
                New York, Museum of Modern Art, 1947, Alfred Stieglitz: His Collection, no. 104.

JEAN FOUQUET   Tours about 1420 – Tours 1477/81

51   Portrait of an Ecclesiastic

Metalpoint and a little black chalk on white prepared paper. $7^{13}/_{16} \times 5^{5}/_{16}$ in. (19.8 × 13.5 cm.)
Inscription in metalpoint at upper right corner: *Ung Roumain legat de na . . . St pere en France*.

Rogers Fund, 49.38

The artist has given us a clue to the identity of the model of this powerful portrait drawing in an inscription that can be translated "A Roman, legate of our Holy Father in France." Henri Bouchot suggested that the legate was Teodoro Lelli, bishop of Treviso, who in 1464, at the age of forty, accompanied the bishop of Ostia to France on a mission to Louis XI. Hulin de Loo, at the beginning of this century, was the first scholar to propose the attribution for this now celebrated sheet to Jean Fouquet. The attribution has been generally accepted, though it has curiously been objected that the psychological characterization is more intense and immediate than in Fouquet's monumental portraits. The only certain drawing by Fouquet is the chalk head of Guillaume Jouvenel des Ursins in the Berlin print room, a study for the panel in the Louvre. The Metropolitan's metalpoint drawing seems stylistically and psychologically compatible with the Berlin drawing, though they differ in technique. Until an alternative solution can be convincingly proposed, the attribution to Fouquet may be accepted. What has never been questioned is the quality of this splendid drawing, one of the finest surviving portrait heads of the fifteenth century. If, as the inscription suggests, the drawing is indeed French, it is difficult to imagine what other artist of the period in France would have been capable of such simple, authoritative draughtsmanship. A red chalk copy, probably dating from the sixteenth century, is in the Royal Collection at Windsor Castle.

PROVENANCE: Prosper Henry Lankrink (Lugt 2090); J. P. Heseltine (Lugt 1507); Henry Oppenheimer, London; Oppenheimer sale, London, Christie's, July 10–14, 1936, no. 428, ill.; Lord Duveen; purchased by the Metropolitan Museum in New York in 1949.

BIBLIOGRAPHY: Sidney Colvin, *Vasari Society*, Part IX, 1913–1914, no. 25, ill.
Klaus G. Perls, *Jean Fouquet*, Paris, 1940, p. 22, pl. 282.
Charles Jacques [Sterling], *La Peinture française. Les Peintres du moyen âge*, Paris, 1941, p. 18, no. 6 (du répétoire), p. 54.
Tietze, *European Master Drawings*, p. 10, no. 5, ill. p. 11.
Grete Ring, *A Century of French Painting 1400–1500*, London, 1949, p. 214, no. 139, pl. 92.
Mongan, *One Hundred Drawings*, p. 12, ill. p. 13.
Shoolman and Slatkin, *French Drawings*, p. 4, pl. 2.

EXHIBITIONS: Paris, Palais du Louvre/Bibliothèque Nationale, 1904, Exposition des primitifs français, no. 44.
London, Grafton Galleries, 1909–1910, National Loan Exhibition, no. 119.
London, Royal Academy, 1932, Exhibition of French Art 1200–1900, no. 541.
Paris, Palais National des Arts, 1937, Chefs-d'oeuvre de l'art français, no. 437.
Philadelphia Museum of Art, 1950–1951, Masterpieces of Drawing, no. 10, ill.

JEAN COUSIN the Elder Sens about 1490 – Paris about 1561
or
JEAN COUSIN the Younger Sens about 1522 – Paris about 1594

52 The Adoration of the Shepherds

Pen and brown ink, brown wash, heightened with white gouache, over black chalk, on brownish paper. 9¹⁵⁄₁₆ × 15⁵⁄₁₆ in. (25.2 × 38.9 cm.)   Rogers Fund, 61.24

Felice Stampfle was the first to point out that this drawing, attributed in the nineteenth century to the Antwerp mannerist Frans Floris, is by the same hand as two drawings bearing old inscriptions that record the name of Jean Cousin. The first of these, representing Jupiter and Semele, is in the British Museum; it is inscribed on the recto *Jehan Cousin* (ill. Jean Adhémar, *Le Dessin français au XVIᵉ siècle,* Lausanne, 1954, p. 99). The second drawing, a study of the apostle Luke in the Pierpont Morgan Library in New York, is inscribed on the verso *Cousin*. Charles Sterling has independently attributed our drawing to Jean Cousin the Younger, calling attention to its connection with a group of drawings published by Otto Benesch as the work of Cousin the Younger (*Prométhée—L'Amour de l'art*, new series, no. 9–10, December 1939–January 1940). Both Jean Cousin the Elder and his son Jean the Younger are recorded to have been successful artists active in Paris, but very little of the work of either of them has survived. However, the style of the present drawing, in which a highly personal calligraphy combines motifs of both Italian and Netherlandish origin, is perfectly compatible with what we know of the two artists. We rediscover this linear style in a series of emblem drawings by Cousin the Younger, the *Livre de Fortune,* dated 1568, in the Bibliothèque de l'Institut in Paris (reproduced in full by L. Lalanne, *Le Livre de Fortune,* Paris and London, 1883). However, in these emblem drawings the draughtsmanship has a derivative, imitative uncertainty that might suggest that Jean the Younger's style derives directly from the more authoritative and original style of his father. Another important and unpublished drawing by the same hand as the Metropolitan's drawing is in the Cabinet des Dessins of the Louvre (Inv. 33,427); it represents putti playing in a landscape with ruins and is classed among the anonymous sixteenth century French drawings.

PROVENANCE: Gerard Leembruggen; Leembruggen sale, C. F. Roos, Amsterdam, March 5, 1866, no. 243 (as Frans Floris); Ignatius Franciscus Ellinckhuysen; Ellinckhuysen sale, Frederik Muller, Amsterdam, November 19–20, 1878, no. 125 (as Frans Floris); purchased by the Metropolitan Museum in New York in 1961.

SIMON VOUET Paris about 1590 – Paris 1649

53 St. Louis

Black chalk, heightened with white chalk, on brownish paper. 15⅜ × 11¼ in. (39.1 × 28.6 cm.)

Inscription in pen and brown ink at lower right: *Vouet*.   Rogers Fund, 61.132

Vouet has studied here the sweep of the wind-blown drapery of a figure of St. Louis of France for a large altarpiece representing the Apotheosis of St. Louis, painted for the high altar of the principal Jesuit church in Paris, St. Louis, now St. Paul-et-St. Louis, in the Rue St. Antoine (ill. William R. Crelly, *The Painting of Simon Vouet,* New Haven, 1962, fig. 76). In this altarpiece, presently in the Rouen Museum, St. Louis is represented carried up to heaven by two angels; on a ledge below are displayed the emblems of French royal power. The painting, one of several executed by Vouet for the Parisian Jesuits, was engraved in 1665 by François Tortebat. The style of both the altarpiece and our preparatory drawing suggests a date in the 1640s, toward the end of Vouet's highly successful career as court painter. The treatment of the heavy, elegantly disposed drapery, conceived in ornamental rather than in functional terms, is particularly characteristic of the artist's maturity; and the rich, decorative quality of Vouet's art was to have a preponderant influence in French painting of the seventeenth and the eighteenth centuries.

PROVENANCE: Purchased by the Metropolitan Museum in Paris in 1961.

BIBLIOGRAPHY: J. Bean, *Metropolitan Museum of Art Bulletin,* January 1962, ill. p. 169, fig. 13.

Douet

NICOLAS POUSSIN Les Andelys 1594 – Rome 1665

54 The Entombment

Pen and brown ink. 3⁷⁄₁₆ × 6⅛ in. (8.8 × 15.6 cm.)

Inscription in pen and brown ink at lower right: *nicolas P . . .*   Rogers Fund, 61.123.1

The masterful balance of the composition suggests, as does the trembling pen line of certain passages, that this drawing dates from Poussin's mature years. Much earlier, about 1630, he had painted a Mourning over the Dead Christ, now in the Alte Pinakothek at Munich (ill. O. Grautoff, *Nicolas Poussin,* Munich, 1914, no. 20); this early representation is impassioned and baroque. At least twenty years later he painted an Entombment, a solemn classical composition where the compositional accents are all vertical and horizontal; this is now in the National Gallery of Ireland at Dublin (ill. Anthony Blunt, *Exposition Nicolas Poussin,* Paris, Musée du Louvre, 1960, no. 96). Blunt first dated the Dublin picture about 1650, and Denis Mahon has proposed 1654–1656 (Mahon, *Poussiniana,* Paris, 1962, p. 29). The dating of Poussin's drawings is even more difficult than the chronology of his pictures, but it might be suggested that our drawing is an early scheme for the Dublin picture. In the drawn composition the diagonal accent of the dead Christ's body unifies the design in an exceptionally satisfying way, and the fervent gestures of the participants in the tragic scene all serve in the construction of a monumental bas-relief.

PROVENANCE: Purchased by the Metropolitan Museum in London in 1961.

BIBLIOGRAPHY: J. Bean, *Metropolitan Museum of Art Bulletin,* January 1962, ill. p. 168, fig. 11.

CLAUDE GILLOT Langres 1673 – Paris 1722

55 Four Figures in Theatrical Costumes

Pen and brown ink, red chalk. 5½ × 7⅞ in. (13.8 × 20 cm.)   Rogers Fund, 10.45.15

The four figures sketched on this sheet wear costumes typical of the *commedia dell'arte,* the *comédie italienne* that inspired so much of Gillot's work. The artist was not only influenced by the theater, but he also designed costumes for ballets, operas, and comedies. Just a few years after Gillot's death, his pupil the engraver Joullain issued a series of eighty-five etchings recording his master's costume designs. Most of these are said to have been designs for the costumes worn in the *Ballet des Quatre Éléments* given at the Palais des Tuileries on December 31, 1721, in which Louis XV, then eleven years old, himself danced. The Cabinet des Dessins at the Louvre possesses one of Gillot's original drawings reproduced in Joullain's etched series (Inv. 26,763, studies for the costumes of *Le Temps* and *Plutus;* the etchings are recorded in Populus's *Gillot* as nos. 395, 399, 437, and 439). The style of the Louvre sheet is very close to that of the Metropolitan Museum's drawing, though the costumes studied on our sheet were not etched by Joullain. Other drawings offer similarly disposed sketches of costumes for the *comédie italienne*: a further sheet in the Metropolitan Museum (06.1042.7) and a drawing formerly in the collection of Marius Paulme (see Paulme sale catalogue, Paris, May 13, 1929, no. 93, pl. 63).

PROVENANCE: Jonathan Richardson junior (Lugt 2170); purchased by the Metropolitan Museum in London in 1909.

ANTOINE WATTEAU Valenciennes 1684 – Nogent-sur-Marne 1721

56 Study of a Man's Head

Red and black chalk. 5⅞ × 5⅛ in. (14.9 × 13 cm.) Surface of sheet slightly damaged at center.
Rogers Fund, 37.165.107

This sensitively modeled head must be a preparatory study for the face of the figure of Mezzetin, represented seated in a garden and strumming a guitar, in a celebrated picture that passed from the collection of Watteau's patron, Jean de Julienne, to the Hermitage and then in 1934 to the Metropolitan Museum (ill. Sterling, *French Paintings,* p. 107). The valet Mezzetin was a stock figure in the *commedia dell'arte* so fashionable in early eighteenth century Paris, and Watteau delighted in drawing and painting his friends in the costumes of the Italian comedy. Unsuccessful attempts have been made to identify the Mezzetin of the Metropolitan's picture and drawing as Angelo Constantini or Luigi Riccoboni, both well-known Italian actors, but it seems more likely that Watteau has posed an unidentified friend or professional model as Mezzetin. With a few variants the correspondence between the heads in the drawing and in the painting is very close and convincing. The picture may be dated quite late in Watteau's brief career, about 1719, and quite close to the Berlin Museum's Enseigne de Gersaint; the style of the drawing is entirely compatible with this date.

PROVENANCE: Jules Niel (Lugt 1944); Marquis de Biron, Paris and Geneva, who purchased it from Niel's daughter; Biron sale, Paris, Galerie Georges Petit, June 9–11, 1914, no. 63; re-entered Biron Collection after sale; purchased by the Metropolitan Museum in Geneva in 1937.

BIBLIOGRAPHY: Josephine L. Allen, "Drawings from the Biron Collection," *Metropolitan Museum of Art Bulletin,* March 1938, pp. 77–78, ill. p. 77.
H. W. Williams, Jr., "Some French Drawings from the Biron Collection," *Art Quarterly,* II, no. 1, Winter 1939, p. 51, fig. 2.
Metropolitan Museum, *European Drawings,* II, ill. no. 31.
Tietze, *European Master Drawings,* p. 166, no. 83, ill. p. 167.
Shoolman and Slatkin, *French Drawings,* p. 42, pl. 25.
K. T. Parker and J. Mathey, *Catalogue de l'oeuvre dessiné d'Antoine Watteau,* II, Paris, 1957, p. 339, no. 726, ill.

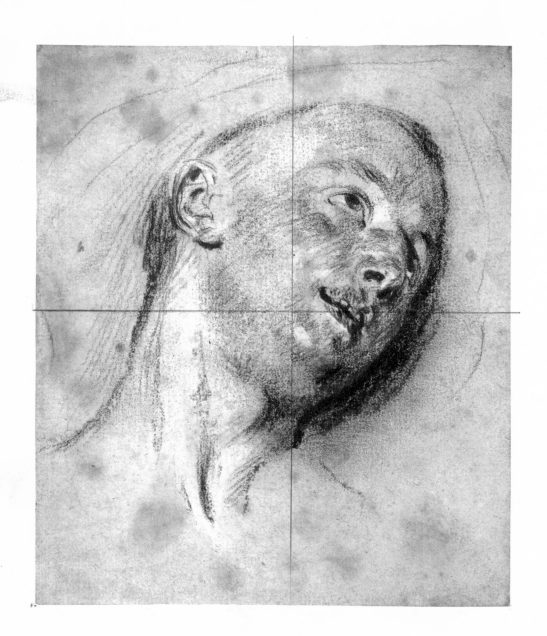

JEAN-BAPTISTE OUDRY Paris 1686 – Beauvais 1755

57 View in the Gardens of Arcueil

Black and white chalk on blue paper. 12⅝₁₆ × 20½ in. (31.4 × 52.1 cm.)
Signed and dated in pen and brown ink at lower left: *JB oudry 1744*

Rogers Fund, 10.45.28

Oudry had access to the celebrated gardens of Anne-Marie-Joseph de Lorraine, called the
Prince de Guise, at Arcueil near Paris. These visits are recorded in a whole series of black
and white chalk drawings on blue paper, close in style to the Metropolitan's sheet and vari-
ously dated 1744, 1745, and 1747. The Louvre, the École des Beaux-Arts, and the Musée
Carnavalet in Paris, the Musée de l'Île de France at Sceaux, the Witt Collection in London,
and the Albertina in Vienna all have drawings from this series. These garden views with
"wings" of foliage, where spatial recession is suggested by strong accents of light and
receding trellised fences, look forward to romantic stage settings. In some of them figures
have been added by a later hand; according to Edmond de Goncourt, these additions were
made on the orders of an early nineteenth century dealer who thought they would sell more
easily if he could "peupler leur vide et leur solitude."

PROVENANCE: William Young Ottley (?); purchased by the Metropolitan Museum in London in 1909.

BIBLIOGRAPHY: Michael Benisovich, "The French Drawings of the Metropolitan Museum," *Burlington Magazine,*
LXXXII, March 1943, p. 73.

JEAN-BAPTISTE GREUZE Tournus 1725 – Paris 1805

59 La Femme Colère

Brush, black and gray wash, over a little black chalk. 20½ × 25⅜₆ in. (52.1 × 64 cm.)

Purchase, Joseph Pulitzer Bequest, 61.1.1

The high finish of this masterful drawing would suggest that it was intended for reproduction, and indeed it was engraved in Greuze's lifetime by Robert Gaillard. In Gaillard's engraving the composition, which appears in reverse, is entitled La Femme Colère (The Angry Wife) and is accompanied by some rather lame moralizing verse signed with the initials P.C.: *Lise calmez votre courroux/ Vous cessez d'être Femme, et vous n'êtes plus Mere/ Tout parle ici pour votre Epoux/ Vos filles plus sages que vous/ Remplissent leur devoir, gardent leur caractère/ En réparant vos torts, et consolant leur Pere* (Lise, restrain your anger, you cease to be a woman and you are no longer a mother. Everything speaks in favor of your husband. Your daughters, wiser than you, fulfill their duty, remain good daughters, by repairing your wrongs and consoling their father). The rather melodramatic sentimentality of the subject, so typical of the artist's work, is interpreted with exceptional brilliance; Greuze was unquestionably one of the most competent and original draughtsmen of eighteenth century France.

PROVENANCE: Joseph Joubert (according to old inscription on verso of mount); M. Hesme de Villeneuve; Hesme sale, Paris, March 3–4, 1856, no. 89; purchased by the Metropolitan Museum in Paris in 1961.

BIBLIOGRAPHY: J. Martin and C. Masson, *Catalogue raisonné de l'oeuvre peint et dessiné de Jean-Baptiste Greuze* (in Camille Mauclair, *Jean-Baptiste Greuze,* Paris, n.d.), p. 11, no. 143.

EXHIBITIONS: Paris, Galerie Cailleux, 1951, Le Dessin français de Watteau à Prud'hon, no. 187.

AUGUSTIN PAJOU Paris 1730 – Paris 1809

60 Design for a Vase and Supporting Console

Pen and brown ink, brown wash, over black chalk, heightened with white gouache. 12⁷⁄₁₆ × 7⅛ in. (31.6 × 18.1 cm.)

Signed twice in pen and brown ink at lower right: *Pajou*   Rogers Fund, 37.165.104

Pajou's mastery of monumental sculptural style is apparent in this rich scheme for an ornamental vase. Admirably suited for their decorative roles, the three entwined tritons that form the console and the two satyrs that support the swan-topped vase have an energy and assurance that recall Puget's sculpture in the previous century. This elegant drawing once hung in the *petit salon* of Edmond de Goncourt's house on the Boulevard de Montmorency in Paris. Stylistically it may be dated in the eighth decade of the eighteenth century, as Hylton Thomas has suggested in the Minnesota exhibition catalogue.

PROVENANCE: Alliance des Arts (Lugt 61); Eugène Tondu; Tondu sale, Paris, April 24–26, 1865, no. 373; Edmond and Jules de Goncourt (Lugt 1089); Goncourt sale, Paris, February 15–17, 1897, no. 224; Marquis de Biron, Paris and Geneva; Biron sale, Paris, Galerie Georges Petit, June 9–11, 1914 no. 40; re-entered the Biron Collection after sale; purchased by the Metropolitan Museum in Geneva in 1937.

BIBLIOGRAPHY: Marquis de Chennevières, *Les Dessins de maîtres anciens exposés à l'École des Beaux-Arts en 1879*, Paris, 1880, p. 99.
Edmond de Goncourt, *La Maison d'un artiste. Nouvelle Édition*, I, Paris, 1881, p. 132.
Henri Stein, *Augustin Pajou*, Paris, 1912, pp. 228, 418.
H. W. Williams, Jr., "Some French Drawings from the Biron Collection," *Art Quarterly*, II, no. 1, Winter 1939, p. 52, fig. 5.
Metropolitan Museum, *European Drawings*, II, ill. no. 33.
Michel N. Benisovich, "Drawings of the Sculptor Augustin Pajou in the United States," *Art Bulletin*, XXXV, no. 4, December 1953, p. 298, fig. 8.

EXHIBITIONS: Paris, École des Beaux-Arts, 1879, Dessins de maîtres anciens, no. 563.
Paris, Musée des Arts Décoratifs, 1880, Dessins de décoration et d'ornement de maîtres anciens, no. 291.
Minneapolis, University of Minnesota, 1961, The Eighteenth Century, One Hundred Drawings by One Hundred Artists, no. 65, pl. XVI.

Pajou

CLAUDE MICHEL, called CLODION Nancy 1738 – Paris 1814

61 Two Putti

Black and white chalk on brownish paper. 9³⁄₁₆ × 11³⁄₈ in. (23.3 × 29.3 cm.)

The Elisha Whittelsey Collection, 59.104

These two putti, one holding aloft a bunch of grapes and seated precariously on an over-turned wine pitcher beside which his companion lolls, were probably drawn for a sculptured group symbolizing Autumn. The soft sculptural modeling of the infant bodies is characteristic of Clodion, who made something of a specialty of such allegorical groups, usually executed in terracotta. A good deal of his small sculpture has been preserved, but preparatory sketches such as this one are rare. The sculptor is concerned here with the overall rhythm of his group and the play of light on its surfaces. The almost impossible relation between the torso and the leg of the reclining infant suggests that the artist was experimenting with alternative solutions for the pose of this figure, asking himself if this putto should be stretched out behind the vase, or rather placed to the right in order to widen the triangular shape of the group. The ancestry of Clodion's putti can be traced back to Titian's Bacchanalia, and they resemble most strikingly the plump allegorical infants introduced to French painting and sculpture by Simon Vouet, whose style as a draughtsman is here recalled as well.

PROVENANCE: Loys Delteil; Delteil sale, Paris, November 13, 1917, no. 15; Marius Paulme (Lugt 1910); Paulme sale, Paris, Galerie Georges Petit, May 13, 1929, no. 46, pl. 30; Hon. Irwin Laughlin, Washington, D.C.; Laughlin sale, London, Sotheby's, June 10, 1959, no. 13, pl. 13, bought by the Metropolitan Museum.

JACQUES-LOUIS DAVID Paris 1748 – Brussels 1825

62 Study of a Seated Draped Male Figure

Black chalk, estompe, heightened with white chalk, on brownish paper; squared off in black chalk. 21⅛₁₆ × 16⅝₁₆ in. (53.6 × 41.4 cm.)

Inscription in pencil in artist's hand at lower right corner: *David à son ami chaudet*

Rogers Fund, 61.161.1

This large chalk drawing of the drapery of a seated male figure is a study for the figure of Crito in The Death of Socrates, an important early picture by David purchased by the Metropolitan Museum in 1931 (ill. Sterling, *French Paintings,* p. 193). The classical drapery of the principal figures in this composition, completed in 1787 and exhibited in the Salon of the same year, was elaborated by David in a series of large-scale, indeed almost full-scale, drawings in black and white chalk. Four of these drawings are in Bayonne, another in Dijon, and two further figure studies connected with the picture are in Tours. Most of these drawings were sold at the time of the dispersal of the contents of David's studio in 1828, while ours was given by the artist during his lifetime to his friend the sculptor Antoine-Denis Chaudet. David had made similar elaborate drapery studies, curiously reminiscent of Florentine studio drawings of the late fifteenth century, for another of his major early pictures, The Oath of the Horatii in the Louvre, dated 1784, but he abandoned this practice in later years.

PROVENANCE: Antoine-Denis Chaudet, Paris; purchased by the Metropolitan Museum in London in 1961.

BIBLIOGRAPHY: J. Bean, *Metropolitan Museum of Art Bulletin,* January 1962, ill. p. 171, fig. 16.

David a son ami chaudet

PIERRE-PAUL PRUD'HON Cluny 1758 – Paris 1823

63 The Assumption of the Virgin

Black and white chalk on blue paper. 18⅜ × 11⅞ in. (46.8 × 30.2 cm.)

Rogers Fund, 37.165.105

This exceptionally free and luminous sketch represents the first stage of Prud'hon's plans for the altarpiece of the chapel in the Palais des Tuileries in Paris. The artist received the official commission in 1816, and the large finished canvas was exhibited in the Salon of 1819. From the chapel of the Tuileries the picture went to the Louvre in 1848 (ill. *Musée National du Louvre. Peintures. École française. XIXᵉ Siècle*, IV, Paris, 1962, pl. 587, no. 1517). The dramatic curve, reminiscent of Roman seventeenth century precedents, that leads the eye upward in the drawing has entirely disappeared in the finished picture, where the composition is far less successful. There the proportions are radically changed, and the figure of the Virgin, seen frontally, is over life-size and occupies almost the entire picture plane. The intervention of ecclesiastical censors may account for these changes. An intermediary stage in the development of the altarpiece is recorded in an oil sketch in the Wallace Collection in London (no. 272), which is close to the finished altarpiece except that the Virgin is swept upward above a circle of nude putti. The Grand Chapelain is said to have objected to the pagan nudity of these figures, and they were suppressed in the final version.

PROVENANCE: Charles de Boisfremont (Lugt 353); Boisfremont sale, Paris, April 9, 1870, no. 15; Courtois sale, Paris, March 28, 1876, no. 66; Paul Casimir-Périer; Casimir-Périer sale, Paris, April 26, 1898, no. 63; Casimir-Périer sale, Paris, January 30–February 1, 1899, no. 29; Marquis de Biron, Paris and Geneva; Biron sale, Paris, Galerie Georges Petit, June 9–11, 1914, no. 43; re-entered Biron Collection after sale; purchased by the Metropolitan Museum in Geneva in 1937.

BIBLIOGRAPHY: Edmond de Goncourt, *Catalogue raisonné de l'oeuvre peint, dessiné, et gravé de P. P. Prud'hon*, Paris 1876, p. 92.

Charles Clément, *Prud'hon, sa vie, ses oeuvres, et sa correspondance*, 3rd ed., Paris, 1880, p. 405.

Jean Guiffrey, *L'Oeuvre de Pierre-Paul Prud'hon* ("Archives de l'Art Français," XIII), Paris, 1924, p. 115, no. 318.

H. W. Williams, Jr., "Some French Drawings from the Biron Collection," *Art Quarterly*, II, no. 1, Winter 1939, pp. 52–53, fig. 6.

J. S. Held, "A Forgotten Prud'hon in New York," *Gazette des Beaux-Arts*, sixth series, XXIII, 1943, p. 294, ill. p. 291, fig. 6.

Metropolitan Museum, *European Drawings*, II, ill. no. 35.

Michael Benisovich, "The French Drawings of the Metropolitan Museum," *Burlington Magazine*, LXXXII, 1943, p. 73, pl. II c.

EXHIBITIONS: Paris, École des Beaux-Arts, 1874, Oeuvres de Prud'hon, no. 168.

JEAN-AUGUSTE-DOMINIQUE INGRES
Montauban 1780 – Paris 1867

64   Three Studies of a Male Nude

Lead pencil. 7¾ × 14⁵⁄₁₆ in. (19.7 × 36.4 cm.) Sheet pierced and repaired at left of center; all four corners of sheet trimmed.

Signed in lead pencil at lower left: *Ing.* Inscriptions in artist's hand in lead pencil from left to right: *clair; grande lumière; plus demi teinte; clair.*   Rogers Fund, 19.125.2

A few years after his arrival in Rome in 1806, Ingres was commissioned by the French military governor of the city to supply pictures for the decoration of the Palazzo del Quirinale, which was then destined to serve as Roman residence for Napoleon I. One of the subjects was chosen from Plutarch: Romulus Victorious over Acron, King of the Caeninenses, Carries the Spolia Opima to the Temple of Jupiter. Working in his studio in the tribune of the church of the Trinità dei Monti, Ingres finished and signed the picture in 1812. A drawing by the artist himself now at Bayonne shows him at work on the composition under the frescoed vault of the church (ill. Henry Lapauze, *Ingres, sa vie et son oeuvre,* Paris, 1911, p. 125). The picture was installed in the Quirinal, then removed in 1815 to the Lateran Palace, given by Pius IX in 1857 to Napoleon III, and was finally hung in the Hemicycle at the École des Beaux-Arts in Paris (ill. Wildenstein, *Ingres,* pl. 34).

Three composition studies for the picture are in the Louvre (R.F. 4623, dated 1808; R.F. 1441, dated 1810; R.F. 4171, undated), and another, from the collection of Étienne-François Haro, was recently on the art market. Ingres also made a number of magnificent studies from the nude for the figures of Romulus and his soldiers, as well as for the dead body of Acron. Many of these drawings once belonged, as ours did, to Ingres's friend the painter Édouard Gatteaux. None of the solutions proposed in our drawing for the position of the arms and feet of the dead body of Acron was adopted in the picture, where the corpse is turned out toward the spectator, with the right arm thrown over the chest. This final position is adumbrated in an equally sensitive study from the Gatteaux Collection now at Bayonne. There Ingres, experimenting with alternative positions, has given the dead figure four arms (ill. *Les Dessins de la Collection Léon Bonnat au Musée de Bayonne,* I, Paris, 1925, pl. 78).

PROVENANCE: Édouard Gatteaux; Édouard Dubufe; François Flameng; Flameng sale, Paris, Galerie Georges Petit, May 26–27, 1919, no. 126, bought by the Metropolitan Museum.

BIBLIOGRAPHY: Édouard Gatteaux, *Collection de 120 dessins, croquis et peintures de M. Ingres classés et mis en ordre par son ami Édouard Gatteaux,* I, Paris, n.d., pl. 45.
Bryson Burroughs, "Recent Accessions: Drawings by Ingres," *Metropolitan Museum of Art Bulletin,* November 1919, pp. 246, 247.
Metropolitan Museum, *European Drawings,* II, ill. no. 38.

EXHIBITIONS: Paris, École des Beaux-Arts, 1867, Tableaux, études, peintes, dessins et croquis de J.-A.-D. Ingres, no. 177.
Paris, Galerie Georges Petit, 1911, Exposition Ingres, no. 191.

JEAN-AUGUSTE-DOMINIQUE INGRES
Montauban 1780 – Paris 1867

66 Study of Classical Drapery

Black chalk, estompe, partially squared off in black chalk, on beige paper. 19⅜ × 12⅝ in. (49.2 × 32.1 cm.)

Signed in black chalk at lower left: *Ingres*   Gustavus A. Pfeiffer Fund, 63.66

This is a highly finished and almost full-scale study for the drapery of the figure of Stratonice in the Antiochus and Stratonice now at Chantilly (ill. Wildenstein, *Ingres,* pl. 82). Commissioned by the Duc d'Orléans in 1834 as a pendant to Paul Delaroche's Assassination of the Duc de Guise, this relatively small picture was painted by Ingres in Rome, finished and dated in 1840, and sent in the same year to Paris, where it was exhibited to a large and admiring public at the Palais Royal. The painter's concern over this important commission is evident in the very considerable number of surviving preparatory drawings for the principal protagonists in this brilliant illustration of a romantic anecdote from ancient history. The figure of Stratonice, beautiful stepmother of the love-sick Antiochus, is studied in some twenty drawings, many of which represent her nude, while others are concerned with the fall of her rich drapery. Most of these drawings are at the Musée Ingres in Montauban, but there are studies of Stratonice draped and undraped at the National Gallery of Scotland in Edinburgh, and nude studies of the figure at the Museum Boymans-van Beuningen in Rotterdam and the Musée des Beaux-Arts in Tours. In the Metropolitan Museum's study Stratonice wears, as she does in the picture, an ingeniously suspended mantle, contrived in imitation of classical models. Indeed, every detail of the picture reveals a concern for archaeological accuracy, and the setting, an imaginary reconstruction of a Hellenistic palace interior, was specially designed by the architect Louis-Pierre Baltard. Ingres conceived the picture as a *grande miniature historique.*

The story of Stratonice had long interested Ingres, and a drawing in the Louvre, which dates from the early years of his first sojourn in Rome, records his first treatment of the theme (ill. Jean Alazard, *Musée du Louvre. J.-D. Ingres. Quatorze Dessins,* Paris, n.d., no. 3). The resounding success of the 1840 picture for the Duc d'Orléans led Ingres to paint two variant replicas of the composition, one dated 1860 now in an American private collection, another dated 1866 with the composition reversed now in Montpellier at the Musée Fabre.

PROVENANCE: Étienne-François Haro (Lugt 1241); Jan Heyligers, Rotterdam; purchased by the Metropolitan Museum in Paris in 1963.

BIBLIOGRAPHY: *Un Choix de dessins de Jean-Dominique Ingres,* Paris, 1926, ill. no. 33 (wrongly said to belong to the Musée Ingres at Montauban).
Alazard, *Ingres,* pl. LXXI.
Jacques Mathey, *Ingres. Dessins,* Paris, n.d., no. 42.

EXHIBITIONS: Paris, École des Beaux-Arts, 1867, Tableaux, études peintes, dessins et croquis de J.-A.-D. Ingres, no. 192.

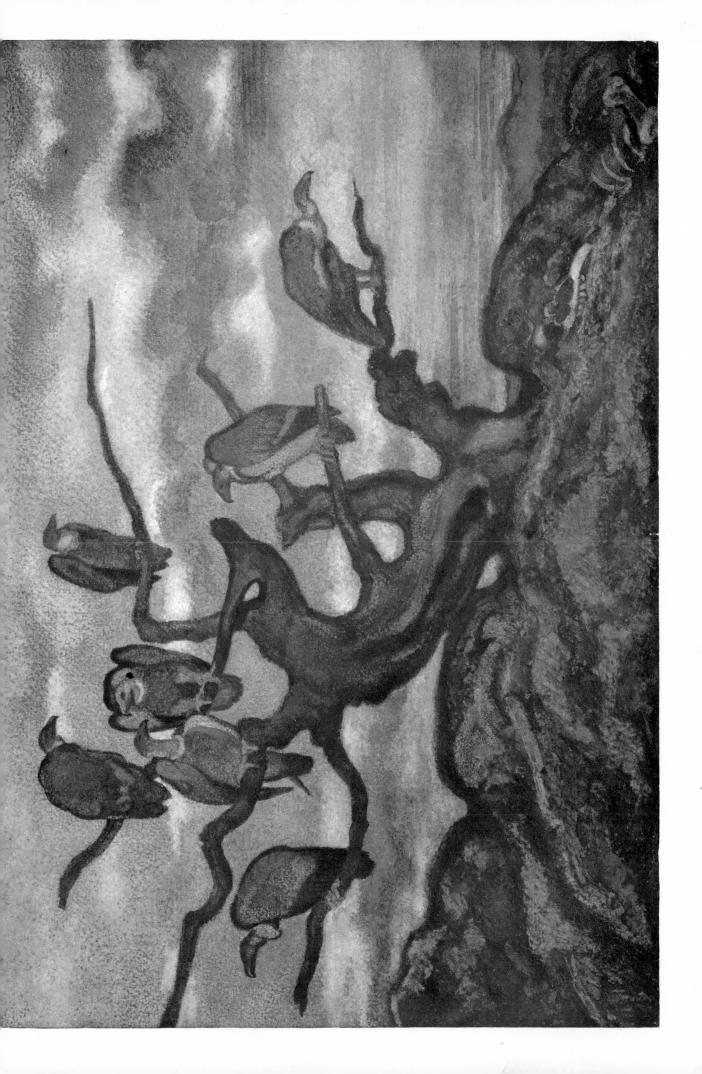

EUGÈNE DELACROIX Charenton-Saint-Maurice 1798 – Paris 1863

68 The Triumph of Genius

Pen and brown ink over lead pencil. 10⅜ × 13¹³⁄₁₆ in. (26.3 × 35.1 cm.)
Inscriptions in pencil at lower center: *Serpent*; at lower right: *plus grand le monstre*
Rogers Fund, 61.160.1

This allegorical subject has been traditionally described as L'Envie or Le Triomphe du Génie. The composition, which harks back to Italian baroque prototypes and is particularly reminiscent of Pietro da Cortona, represents a hero led toward the welcoming figure of Fame by Heroic Virtue, who is identified by Hercules's club. The forces of Envy take form as savage dogs, a clawing tailed monster, and flying armed figures. In another drawing now in the Louvre (R.F. 9362) Delacroix studied a variant scheme for this symbolic composition, and in the Louvre sheet the hero is easily recognizable as Dante. Ten further drawings related to the composition were in the Delacroix sale of 1864. The artist's biographers have dated these studies for an unexecuted allegorical picture about 1840, and have contended that the theme of Genius pursued by Envy was inspired by the artist's bitterness over the rejection of his Le Tasse dans la Maison des Fous by the selection committee of the Salon of 1839.

PROVENANCE: Eugène Delacroix; Delacroix sale (Lugt 838), Paris, February 22–27, 1864, part of no. 378; Alfred Sensier, Paris; Philippe M. Burty, Paris; Burty sale, Paris, March 2–3, 1891, no. 71; Walter Feilchenfeldt, Amsterdam and Zürich; purchased by the Metropolitan Museum in Zürich in 1961.

BIBLIOGRAPHY: Alfred Robaut, *Eugène Delacroix, facsimile de dessins et croquis originaux,* Paris, 1864, pl. 42.
Robaut, *Delacroix,* p. 195, no. 728.
André Michel, "L'Exposition d'Eugène Delacroix à l'École des Beaux-Arts," *Gazette des Beaux-Arts,* 2eme période, XXI, 1885, no. 1, ill. p. 305.
Étienne Moreau-Nélaton, *Delacroix raconté par lui-même,* I, Paris, 1916, p. 197, fig. 179.
J. Bean, *Metropolitan Museum of Art Bulletin,* January 1962, p. 172, fig. 17.
Sérullaz, *Mémorial,* no. 294.

EXHIBITIONS: Paris, École Nationale des Beaux-Arts, 1885, Eugène Delacroix, no catalogue number.
Venice, Esposizione Internazionale d'Arte (28th Biennale), 1956, Eugène Delacroix, no. 70.
Paris, Petit Palais, 1959, De Géricault à Matisse, chefs-d'oeuvre français des collections suisses, no. 158.
Paris, Musée du Louvre, 1963, Centenaire d'Eugène Delacroix, no. 297.

EUGÈNE DELACROIX Charenton-Saint-Maurice 1798 – Paris 1863

69 The Sultan of Morocco before his Palace at Meknès

Lead pencil, squared off in white chalk, on beige paper. 23½ × 19⁹⁄₁₆ in. overall (59.8 × 49.7 cm.) Horizontal strip added at top and drawing continued in the artist's hand.

Rogers Fund, 61.202

In January of 1832 Delacroix set off from Toulon on a journey to North Africa in the party of the Comte de Mornay, special emissary of Louis-Philippe to the sultan of Morocco. The high point of this diplomatic mission was the ceremonial audience accorded by the sultan, Muley-Abd-er-Rahman, outside the palace at Meknès. Delacroix made several sketches of the splendid event in his Moroccan sketchbook, now in the Louvre; more than ten years later he used these notations for the composition of a large picture commemorating the event. An oil sketch now in a private collection in Paris records the first stages of his planning of the picture. The sultan and his cortege appear at the left, Mornay and his attendants at the right. In the completed picture, exhibited at the Salon of 1845, singled out for the highest praise by Baudelaire and purchased by the state for the Toulouse Museum, the French delegation has been omitted and the vertical composition is dominated by the majestic figure of the sultan on horseback. Our drawing, an exceptionally large and finished composition study, is very close to the Toulouse picture. The sheet is squared for transfer in white chalk, which detracts very little from the unity of surface. The gridiron of squaring extends upward just beyond the summit of the umbrella and does not reach the top of the sheet. The vertical extension of the picture is the same as that of the squaring, and the topmost passage of sky that appears in the drawing has been suppressed.

PROVENANCE: Eugène Delacroix, Paris; Delacroix sale (Lugt 838), Paris, February 22–27, 1864, no. 350; G. Arosa, Paris; Arosa sale, Paris, February 27–28, 1884, no. 131; I. Pereire, Paris; Pereire sale, Paris, June 4, 1937, no. 1; M. Bergaud and family, Paris; purchased by the Metropolitan Museum in New York in 1961.

BIBLIOGRAPHY: Robaut, *Delacroix,* p. 434, no. 1711.
Elie Lambert, *Histoire d'un tableau. L'Abd er Rahman Sultan du Maroc de Delacroix* ("Collection Hespéris," XIV), Paris, 1953, p. 18, note 2.
J. Bean, *Metropolitan Museum of Art Bulletin,* January 1962, p. 173, fig. 19.
Sérullaz, *Mémorial,* no. 349.

EXHIBITIONS: Paris, Musée du Louvre, 1963, Centenaire d'Eugène Delacroix, no. 343, ill.

HONORÉ DAUMIER Marseille 1808 – Valmondois 1879

70 Man Reading in a Garden

Water color over black chalk. 13⁵⁄₁₆ × 10⅝ in. (33.8 × 27 cm.)

Signed in brush and black ink at lower left: *h. Daumier*

Verso: Preliminary sketch in pen and brown ink, black chalk, and gray wash for the same
composition.

> Bequest of Mrs. H. O. Havemeyer, 29.100.199, The H. O. Havemeyer Collection

This particularly luminous and transparent water color, representing a man reading with
a hat pulled down to shade his eyes, has been described in all recent literature on Daumier
as a portrait of the artist's friend Corot and, even more specifically, as Corot sketching.
However, K. E. Maison has very recently pointed out that there is no tradition that can
justify this identification. A preparatory sketch for our drawing in a Parisian private collection (ill. K. E. Maison, *Burlington Magazine,* XCVI, January 1954, fig. 8) clearly represents
a man reading, not sketching; this drawing was exhibited during Daumier's lifetime, and
shortly after the death of his famous friend, as Le Liseur, with no mention of Corot. The
Metropolitan's drawing was exhibited in the Daumier exhibition at the École des Beaux-
Arts in 1901 as La Lecture. Both drawings figure under the vague descriptive title of Le
Liseur in Arsène Alexandre's 1888 list of the artist's work, and Alexandre had obtained all
his essential information from Daumier's widow. Maison is surely correct in suggesting
that if the drawing represented as celebrated a figure as Corot, the sources just cited would
have made mention of the important fact. The source of the erroneous modern identification is uncertain.

PROVENANCE: Paul Gallimard, Paris; Durand-Ruel, Paris; H. O. Havemeyer, New York.

BIBLIOGRAPHY: Klossowski, *Daumier,* p. 122, no. 397, pl. 148.
Escholier, *Daumier,* ill. before p. 175.
Fuchs, *Daumier,* p. 53, no. 175, pl. 175.
Rosenthal, *Daumier,* pp. 111–112, pl. XLVIII.
Metropolitan Museum, *European Drawings,* II, ill. no. 44.
Shoolman and Slatkin, *French Drawings,* p. 148, pl. 84.
Adhémar, *Daumier,* pp. 119–120, no. 67, pl. 67.
Adhémar, *Daumier. Dessins,* ill. no. 12.

EXHIBITIONS: Paris, École des Beaux-Arts, 1901, Exposition Daumier, no. 200.
New York, Museum of Modern Art, 1930, Corot-Daumier, no. 122, ill. p. 24.
New York, Metropolitan Museum of Art, 1930, The H. O. Havemeyer Collection, Temporary
Exhibition, no. 142, ill.
Paris, Musée de l'Orangerie, 1934, Daumier, no. 146.
Philadelphia Museum of Art, 1937, Daumier, no. 21, ill.
Paris, Musée de l'Orangerie, 1955, De David à Toulouse-Lautrec. Chefs-d'oeuvre des collections
américaines, no. 64, pl. 31.

JEAN-FRANÇOIS MILLET Gréville 1814 – Barbizon 1875

72 Le Repas des Cantonniers

Black chalk, heightened with white gouache, on brownish paper. 10⅞ × 8⅞ in.
 (27.6 × 22.5 cm.)
Signed in black chalk at lower right corner: *J. F. Millet*   Rogers Fund, 26.243.1

The rustic subject studied here is typical of Millet; three road workers, silhouetted against the skyline, relax as they eat their meal. In the foreground their abandoned tools lie in the road trench they have been digging. The composition, with a plunging view down on the road and a high-placed horizon line is, on the other hand, unusual for Millet, and most original and felicitous. No painted version of the subject is recorded, but Millet studied the theme in another drawing. In a sheet now in the Ashmolean Museum at Oxford a similar group of three road workers appear, two of them seated and one standing in the excavated road (ill. *Studio,* LIX, 1913, p. 100). Robert Herbert has suggested a date between 1850 and 1852 for our drawing.

PROVENANCE: Alfred Sensier; Sensier sale, Paris, December 11–12, 1877, no. 231; Jules Ferry; Ferry sale, Paris, February 11–12, 1921, no. 69, pl. 69; purchased by the Metropolitan Museum in New York in 1926.

ÉDOUARD MANET Paris 1832 – Paris 1883

73 A Man on Crutches

Brush and black ink on tan paper. 10⅝ × 7¾ in. (27.1 × 19.7 cm.)
Monogram in brush and black ink at center of lower margin: *M.*   Dick Fund, 48.10.2

It is said that Manet made this brilliant brush drawing as an illustration for a song, "L'Homme aux béquilles," composed by a popular dance-hall musician called Cabaner. The song never seems to have been published, but the same one-legged figure appears in reverse in one of Manet's pictures. We can recognize him, dressed in the same workman's blouse, hobbling up the street, in La Rue Mosnier aux Drapeaux, a picture signed and dated 1878, now in the collection of Paul Mellon (ill. Paul Jamot and Georges Wildenstein, *Manet,* II, Paris, 1932, fig. 323). A pen sketch of the man on crutches, inscribed *au moment de la fête,* is at Oxford in the Ashmolean Museum (ill. Mathey, II, fig. 71).

PROVENANCE: Mme veuve Manet (Lugt 880); Manet atelier sale, Paris, February 4–5, 1884, no. 154; sale, Paris April 24, 1944; purchased by the Metropolitan Museum in Paris in 1948.

BIBLIOGRAPHY: Edmond Bazire, *Manet,* Paris, 1884, ill. p. 81.
Étienne Moreau-Nélaton, *Manet raconté par lui-même,* II, Paris, 1926, fig. 231.
A. Tabarant, *Manet. Histoire catalographique,* Paris, 1931, p. 545, no. 71.
A. Tabarant, *Manet et ses oeuvres,* Paris, 1947, p. 325, ill. p. 621, fig. 623.
J. Mathey, *Graphisme de Manet,* II, *Peintures réapparues,* Paris, 1963, p. 17, fig. 70.

EXHIBITIONS: Paris, École des Beaux-Arts, 1884, Oeuvres d'Édouard Manet, no. 174.

'EDGAR-HILAIRE-GERMAIN DEGAS Paris 1834 – Paris 1917

74 Portrait of Édouard Manet

Black chalk and estompe. 13 × 9⅛ in. (33 × 23 cm.)   Rogers Fund, 19.51.7

About 1864 Degas made two etched portraits of the painter Édouard Manet (ill. Loys Delteil, *Le Peintre-graveur illustré*, IX, *Degas,* Paris, 1919, nos. 15, 16). In the first of these Manet is seated, with his *chapeau haut-de-forme* in hand. The present drawing and another sketch in the Metropolitan Museum (19.51.6), both of them purchased at the sale of the contents of Degas's studio in 1918, are preparatory studies for this etching, where the figure appears in reverse. A drawing in the Rouart Collection in Paris is a study for the second etching, where Manet is seated with his hands folded. The artist is also portrayed watching the races at Longchamps in a further drawing in the Museum's collection (19.51.8). Manet and Degas seem to have been good friends, in spite of the latter's rather irascible nature and a mutual professional suspicion. About the time these drawings were made, Degas painted Manet listening to Mme Manet playing the piano. Manet, to whom Degas presented the picture, was dissatisfied with his wife's likeness and cut her off the canvas—a mutilation that quite understandably enraged Degas.

PROVENANCE: Atelier Degas (Lugt 657); second Degas atelier sale (Lugt 658), Galerie Georges Petit, Paris, December 11–13, 1918, part of no. 210, bought by the Metropolitan Museum.

BIBLIOGRAPHY: Bryson Burroughs, "Drawings by Degas," *Metropolitan Museum of Art Bulletin,* May 1919, p. 115, ill. p. 116.
Metropolitan Museum, *European Drawings,* II, ill. no. 49.
Tietze, *European Master Drawings,* p. 286, no. 143, ill. p. 287.
Rich, *Degas,* ill. p. 18.

EXHIBITIONS: Paris, Musée de l'Orangerie, 1955, De David à Toulouse-Lautrec. Chefs-d'oeuvre des collections américaines, no. 67, pl. 61.

Degas

EDGAR-HILAIRE-GERMAIN DEGAS Paris 1834 – Paris 1917

75 Portrait of Edmond Duranty

Charcoal, heightened with white chalk, on blue paper. 12⅛ × 18⅝ in. (30.8 × 47.2 cm.)

Rogers Fund, 19.51.9a

A somewhat forgotten naturalistic novelist, Edmond Duranty was a literary figure of considerable importance in the history of impressionism. His brochure *La Nouvelle Peinture: à propos d'un groupe d'artistes qui expose dans les Galeries Durand-Ruel* (Paris, 1876) was the first publication to deal seriously with the impressionist group. An habitué of the Café Guerbois, Duranty knew all the members of the impressionist circle, but he seems to have been particularly close to Degas. Duranty sought the subjects of his novels in everyday life, and he recognized in Degas's analytical realism a pictorial counterpart to his literary program. Indeed, Duranty's formulation of a realistic program comes so close to Degas's own rare theoretical pronouncements that it has even been said that the painter himself was largely responsible for Duranty's brochure. Degas's portrait of Duranty was undertaken a few years after the publication of the brochure; the finished picture, now in the Glasgow Art Gallery, is dated 1879 (ill. P. A. Lemoisne, *Degas,* II, Paris, 1946, pl. 517). A large pastel version, presumably made in advance of and in preparation for the canvas, is in the collection of Mrs. Julian C. Eisenstein at Washington, D.C. (ill. Lemoisne, *Degas,* pl. 518). In both these versions Duranty is represented seated behind a writing table on which he rests his left elbow, against a background of books. The present drawing and the study of bookshelves (pl. 76) record Degas's search for the linear structure of the picture; the solution arrived at here satisfied the very exigent draughtsman and was used with little change in the portrait.

PROVENANCE: Atelier Degas (Lugt 657); second Degas atelier sale (Lugt 658), Paris, Galerie Georges Petit, December 11–13, 1918, part of no. 242, bought by the Metropolitan Museum.

BIBLIOGRAPHY: Bryson Burroughs, "Drawings by Degas," *Metropolitan Museum of Art Bulletin,* May 1919, pp. 115–116, ill. p. 117.
Metropolitan Museum, *European Drawings,* II, ill. no. 52.
Rich, *Degas,* ill. p. 11.

EDGAR-HILAIRE-GERMAIN DEGAS Paris 1834 – Paris 1917

76   Bookshelves

Charcoal, heightened with white chalk, on brownish paper. 18½ × 12 in. (46.9 × 30.5 cm.)
Rogers Fund, 19.51.9b

The bookshelves and the pile of papers so masterfully studied here occur as an emblematic background in the portrait of Edmond Duranty (pl. 75) seated at his writing desk. Duranty is there seen in an informal setting where shelves of books in disorder identify him at once as a man of letters. The Duranty portrait dates from 1879; some ten years earlier Manet painted Émile Zola seated at a writing desk in disarray, with a Japanese print and reproductions of pictures by Velazquez and Manet stuck in a picture frame on the wall above. The accessories in both Manet's Zola and Degas's Duranty strike that note of modernism, of up-to-dateness, in the search for which the two painters rivaled each other. However, in Degas's portrait the casually posed but strikingly monumental figure of Duranty so dominates the composition that the books behind play only a subservient decorative and heraldic role. This portrait, for all of its contemporary savor, rejoins the tradition of the humanist portrait of the Renaissance; yet it looks forward to Cézanne's portrait of Gustave Geffroy (Pellerin Collection, Paris), painted in 1895, where the pose of the sitter and the background of books seem directly derived from Degas's composition.

PROVENANCE: Atelier Degas (Lugt 657); second Degas atelier sale (Lugt 658), Paris, Galerie Georges Petit, December 11–13, 1918, part of no. 242, bought by the Metropolitan Museum.

BIBLIOGRAPHY: Bryson Burroughs, "Drawings by Degas," *Metropolitan Museum of Art Bulletin,* May 1919, p. 116.

GEORGES SEURAT Paris 1859 – Paris 1891

78 Portrait of Edmond-François Aman-Jean

Conté crayon. 24½ × 18¾ in. (62.2 × 47.6 cm.)

Signed and dated in conté crayon at upper right: *Seurat 1883* (signature visible only under ultraviolet light).

Bequest of Stephen C. Clark, 61.101.16

Seurat attached great importance to his drawings and exhibited them with his pictures as independent works of art. This monumental portrait of his friend the painter Aman-Jean is his largest and probably most important drawing; it is a manifesto of the independence of draughtsmanship. Not a preparatory study for a painted portrait, the drawing is a finished and definitive work, where the rich textured effects of conté crayon, thickly and painstakingly applied, conjure up the subtlest pictorial effects. Edmond-François Aman-Jean was a fellow student of Seurat's at the École Municipale du Dessin and the École des Beaux-Arts in Paris, and in 1879 they shared a studio together. This portrait, signed and dated 1883, was shown at the Salon the same year; it was the first work by the artist to figure in a public exhibition.

PROVENANCE: Edmond-François Aman-Jean; Stephen C. Clark, New York.

BIBLIOGRAPHY: Seligman, *Seurat,* p. 72, no. 42, pl. XXXI.
Tietze, *European Master Drawings,* p. 296, no. 148, ill. p. 297.
Mongan, *One Hundred Drawings,* p. 184, ill. p. 185.
De Hauke, *Seurat,* II, p. 166, no. 588, ill. p. 167 (with previous bibliography and complete list of exhibitions).
Herbert, *Seurat's Drawings,* pp. 135–136, fig. 115.

EXHIBITIONS: Paris, Salon des Indépendants, 1883, no. 3189 (this catalogue entry refers to Seurat's portrait of his mother, pl. 77, but the Aman-Jean was in fact exhibited under this number).
Paris, Musée de l'Orangerie, 1955, De David à Toulouse-Lautrec. Chefs-d'oeuvre des collections américaines, no. 89, pl. 92.
Chicago, Art Institute/New York, Museum of Modern Art, 1958, Seurat. Paintings and Drawings, no. 38, ill.
Rotterdam/Paris/New York, 1958–1959, From Clouet to Matisse. French Drawings from American Collections, no. 185, pl. 184.

JACQUES VILLON Damville 1875 – Cannes 1963

79 Portrait of Félix Barré

Black chalk over slight traces of blue pencil. 14¾ × 13⁵⁄₁₆ in. overall (36.8 × 33.8 cm.) The surface of the drawing as reproduced measures 9¼ × 8⅛ in.

Signed and dated in lead pencil at right: *Jacques Villon 12*   Rogers Fund, 63.4

The energetic stylization of this head, the planes of which are treated abstractly like the facets of a cut stone, reveals Villon's nearness to cubism at a decisive stage of his career. After working for over ten years as a commercial illustrator, he began to paint seriously in 1910, at the age of thirty-five. This drawing, a study for an engraving, dates from 1912, the year of the Section d'Or exhibition in Paris, an important manifestation of which Villon was one of the organizers and in which he exhibited. The massive, rocklike head of the actor Félix Barré was studied and analyzed by Villon in a group of works in the years 1912–1913. In addition to the engraving for which our drawing was prepared, he made a drypoint, where the head is treated more naturalistically, and a drypoint of the head and shoulders of Barré that, on the contrary, pushes the abstraction beyond the limits attained in the present drawing (ill. Jacqueline Auberty and Charles Pérussaux, *Jacques Villon, catalogue de son oeuvre gravé*, Paris, 1950, nos. 190, 189, 199 respectively). Three painted portraits of Barré date from the same years (ill. Dora Vallier, *Jacques Villon, oeuvres de 1897 à 1956,* Paris, n.d., pp. 40–41).

PROVENANCE: Louis Macmillan; purchased by the Metropolitan Museum in New York in 1963.

EXHIBITIONS: New York, Solomon R. Guggenheim Museum/Minneapolis, University Gallery/Cambridge, Fogg Art Museum, 1963–1964, Twentieth Century Master Drawings, no. 119, pl. 19.

Jacpus Villon
12

ALBRECHT DÜRER Nuremberg 1471 – Nuremberg 1528

80 St. Catherine

Pen and dark brown ink. 6½ × 2¹⁵⁄₁₆ in. (16.5 × 7.4 cm.) Lower left corner replaced.
Verso: Illegible black chalk sketch.   Rogers Fund, 19.75

Panofsky has suggested that this drawing may be Dürer's study for the figure of St. Catherine as she appeared on one of the fixed wings of the Paumgärtner altarpiece now in the Alte Pinakothek in Munich. He further relates a pen study for a St. Barbara in the Museum Boymans-van Beuningen at Rotterdam (ill. Winkler, fig. 194) with the figure that occupied the other fixed wing. These sections of the altarpiece have disappeared, and only the central panel with a representation of the Nativity and the movable shutters with figures of St. George and St. Catherine, traditionally said to represent the brothers Lucas and Stephan Paumgärtner, are preserved in Munich (ill. Panofsky, II, fig. 111). The Paumgärtner altarpiece was probably executed between 1502 and 1504, and Panofsky dates our drawing and the Rotterdam sketch about 1500. Winkler, who did not connect the Metropolitan drawing with the altarpiece, suggested an even earlier dating.

PROVENANCE: Thomas Banks (Lugt 2423); Mrs. Edward Foster, London; Ambrose Poynter (Lugt 161); Sir Edward J. Poynter (Lugt 874); Poynter sale, London, Sotheby's, April 25, 1918, no. 244, bought by the Metropolitan Museum.

BIBLIOGRAPHY: Campbell Dodgson, *Vasari Society,* Part VI, 1910–1911, no. 24, ill.
Bryson Burroughs, *Metropolitan Museum of Art Bulletin,* June 1919, p. 138, ill. p. 139.
Friedrich Lippmann, *Zeichnungen von Albrecht Dürer,* VI, ed. Friedrich Winkler, Berlin, 1927, no. 682.
H. Tietze and E. Tietze-Conrat, *Kritische Verzeichnis der Werke Albrecht Dürers,* I, Augsburg, 1928, p. 130, no. A 148; II, Part 2, Basel and Leipzig, 1938, p. 132, no. A 392, ill. p. 266 (the drawing not accepted as Dürer's work and attributed to the circle of Kulmbach).
Friedrich Winkler, *Die Zeichnungen Albrecht Dürers,* I, Berlin, 1936, p. 66, no. 90, fig. 90.
Metropolitan Museum, *European Drawings,* II, ill. no. 15.
Erwin Panofsky, *Albrecht Dürer,* 3rd ed., Princeton, 1948, I, p. 91; II, p. 89, no. 854.

EXHIBITIONS: New York, Pierpont Morgan Library, 1955, Drawings and Prints by Albrecht Dürer, no. 4.

PETER PAUL RUBENS Siegen 1577 – Antwerp 1640

81 The Garden of Love

Pen and brown ink, brown and green wash, heightened with light blue gouache, over black chalk. 18¾ × 27¹³⁄₁₆ in. (47.7 × 70.7 cm.) Vertical crease at center.

Inscription in pen and brown ink at lower left: *Pietro Paolo Rubbens*

Fletcher Fund, 58.96.2

This magnificent drawing was made by Rubens as a model for a woodcut executed in reverse by Christoffel Jegher; a further drawing by Rubens, also in the Metropolitan Museum, is the model for the pendant woodcut. Each drawing and each woodcut offer a balanced, self-contained design, but the two "halves" combine to form a complete composition of exceptional richness and complexity. The present drawing offers the right extension of the full design; in the reversed woodcut version the putto hovering at the left and the head of the man in plumed hat at the right have been suppressed and the architectural background considerably altered. The left part of the composition, studied in the other Metropolitan Museum drawing, contains two further couples in gallant conversation and a group of ladies and gentlemen surprised by jets of water. Traditionally known as the Garden of Love, the subject of these drawings is perhaps best known through Rubens's picture in the Prado, the composition of which differs in many ways from, though it is certainly related to, the woodcut version. Both Burchard and Held had maintained that the Prado picture preceded our drawings and the woodcuts. The success of the picture, of which many old copies are known, would have led Rubens to design a new version, for wider distribution, of an understandably popular composition. But more recently Burchard, after careful examination of another little-known version of the Garden of Love at Waddesdon Manor, a picture that had been difficult to see until the Rothschild collections at Waddesdon passed to the National Trust, came to the conclusion that this version, though later modified and repainted by the artist himself, was the earliest stage in the evolution of the composition. First came the Waddesdon picture, then about 1630–1632 our drawings for the woodcuts, and immediately thereafter the Prado picture.

PROVENANCE: Possibly Canon Joannes Philippus Happart, Antwerp (both drawings); Pierre Crozat (one of the drawings was in the Crozat sale, Paris, April 10–May 13, 1741, no. 828, purchased by Mariette, who received the other drawing as a gift from Crozat's nephew, the Baron de Thiers); Pierre-Jean Mariette; Mariette sale, Paris, November 15, 1775, no. 994 (both drawings); Jan Gildemeester, Amsterdam; Gildemeester sale, Amsterdam, November 24, 1800, Konst Boek B. I, N. 3; Hendrik van Eyl-Sluyter, Amsterdam; Eyl-Sluyter sale, Amsterdam, September 26, 1814, portfolio N, no. 1; Heneage Finch, 5th Earl of Aylesford (Lugt 58); Aylesford sale, London, Christie's, July 17–18, 1893, no. 272; Sir John Charles Robinson (Lugt 1433); Robinson sale, London, Christie's, May 12–14, 1902, no. 334; William Hesketh, 1st Viscount Leverhulme; Lady Lever Art Gallery, Port Sunlight, Cheshire; purchased by the Metropolitan Museum in London in 1958.

BIBLIOGRAPHY: Julius S. Held, *Rubens, Selected Drawings,* I, London, 1959, p. 153, no. 152 (with previous bibliography); II, pl. 163.
Wolfgang Burchard (from notes left by his father, Ludwig Burchard), "The 'Garden of Love' by Rubens," *Burlington Magazine,* CV, no. 727, October 1963, pp. 428–432.
L. Burchard and R.-A. d'Hulst, *Rubens Drawings,* I, Brussels, 1963, pp. 278–281; II, left and right sections, pl. 180.

EXHIBITIONS: London, New Gallery, 1899–1900, Exhibition of Pictures . . . Including a Selection from the Works of . . . Rubens, no. 150.
London, Wildenstein and Co., 1950, Loan Exhibition of Works by Rubens, no. 47, left half ill.
Antwerp, Rubenshuis, 1956, Tekeningen van P. P. Rubens, no. 128, pl. LVII.

ANTON VAN DYCK Antwerp 1599 – London 1641

82 The Comte d'Arenberg

Pen and brown ink. 9¹⁄₁₆ × 9⅝ in. (23 × 25 cm.)
Inscription in pen and dark brown ink at lower left: *The Count of Arenberg by Vandyke.*
Verso: Pen study of a *Venus pudica* and black chalk sketch of two male figures.

Gift of Harold K. Hochschild, 40.91.16

The old English inscription on the drawing correctly suggests the connection with an equestrian portrait of the Comte d'Arenberg in the collection of the Earl of Leicester at Holkham Hall (Courtauld Institute photo B55/368). In the picture the composition is reversed, and the horse rears up at the left; the cavalier is hatless, and though he wears a similar suit of armor, his scarf is tied around his waist instead of across his shoulder. A youth at the right in the picture holds the cavalier's armored headpiece. A pen sketch of a cavalier in the British Museum (ill. Vey, II, pl. 228) is stylistically similar to our sheet but closer to the Holkham Hall picture. In 1628 Albert de Ligne, Prince de Brabançon et Comte d'Arenberg, was invested with the Order of the Golden Fleece, which he wears conspicuously in the painted portrait. Thus the picture and the two drawings as well must date between that year and 1632, when Van Dyck left Flanders for England. In 1634, not long after the picture had been painted, d'Arenberg was arrested for his part in an alleged conspiracy against Hapsburg rule in the Netherlands.

PROVENANCE: Earls of Pembroke; Pembroke sale, London, Sotheby's, July 5–10, 1917, no. 378; Harold K. Hochschild, New York.

BIBLIOGRAPHY: Strong, *Wilton House Drawings,* Part II, ill. no. 21.
A. E. Popham, "A Drawing by Sir Anthony van Dyck," *British Museum Quarterly,* XII, no. 2, 1938, pp. 49–50.
Metropolitan Museum, *European Drawings,* II, ill. no. 2.
Tietze, *European Master Drawings,* p. 124, no. 62, ill. p. 125.
Horst Vey, *Die Zeichnungen Anton van Dycks,* Brussels, 1962, I, p. 257, no. 187; II, pl. 227.

EXHIBITIONS: Philadelphia Museum of Art, 1950–1951, Masterpieces of Drawing, no. 56, ill.
Antwerp, Rubenshuis/Rotterdam, Museum Boymans-van Beuningen, 1960, Antoon van Dyck, Tekeningen en Olieverfschetsen, no. 88, pl. LVII.

...t of Arenberg by Vandyke

HENDRICK GOLTZIUS Venlo 1558 – Haarlem 1617

83 Autumn

Pen and brown ink, red-brown wash, over black chalk, heightened with a little white gouache. 7⅝ × 5¹¹⁄₁₆ in. (19.4 × 14.5 cm.)

Monogram in pen and brown ink on barrel at right: HG   Rogers Fund, 61.25.2

Goltzius suggests the mood of autumn by representing a prudent housewife gathering fruit and squash for winter storage. A youth crowned like Bacchus with grapes, about to taste of the year's wine, is interrupted by a sinister gentleman who may symbolize the yearly death that winter brings. In the sky we can discern birds flying away to the south. This drawing was one of a series of four compositions representing the seasons that were engraved in reverse by Jan Saenredam (Bartsch, III, p. 258, nos. 119–122). Only two of Goltzius's original designs have survived; the drawings for Summer and Winter are presumably lost, but the Metropolitan Museum possesses the drawing for Spring, where amorous couples engage in gallant discourse in a garden (ill. Reznicek, no. 155, pl. 304). Reznicek dates these drawings about 1597.

PROVENANCE: Henry Scipio Reitlinger, London; Reitlinger sale, London, Sotheby's, June 22–23, 1954, no. 657; N. Beets, Amsterdam; purchased by the Metropolitan Museum in Boston in 1961.

BIBLIOGRAPHY: E. K. J. Reznicek, *Die Zeichnungen von Hendrick Goltzius,* Utrecht, 1961, I, p. 300, no. 156; II, pl. 303.

ABRAHAM BLOEMAERT Dordrecht 1564 – Utrecht 1651

84 Christ and the Adulteress

Pen and brown ink, brown wash, over black chalk, heightened with a little white gouache.
13½ × 18⅞ in. (34.3 × 48 cm.) Vertical crease at center; diagonal creases at left.
Signed and dated in pen and brown ink at lower left margin: *A Bloemart fe 1595*

Rogers Fund, 62.44

Signed and dated 1595, this early Bloemaert drawing shows Dutch mannerism at one of its most convulsive moments. The arbitrary linear style is almost perverse and transforms the protagonists into gesticulating mannequins, but Bloemaert gives an impressive dramatic unity to the composition by contrasting passages of dark wash with white highlights. The shadowed forms silhouetted in the left foreground lead the eye into the flood-lit middle ground where the action takes place. Such a use of contrasting planes of light and dark to give added plasticity and coherence to a design can be encountered in drawings by Dutch artists of the following century; Breenbergh's View of Tivoli (pl. 86) is constructed in just this way. The heavily draped figure seen from the back at the left foreground of Bloemaert's drawing appears in reverse in a picture representing the Baptism of Christ at the National Gallery of Canada in Ottawa (ill. *Catalogue of Paintings and Sculpture,* I, *Older Schools,* Ottawa, 1957, p. 93). The Ottawa picture has been attributed to Bloemaert and more recently to Joachim Wtewael, a painter of the school of Utrecht very close to Bloemaert.

PROVENANCE: Théodore-Charles-Louis Hippert (Lugt 1377); purchased by the Metropolitan Museum in Paris in 1962.

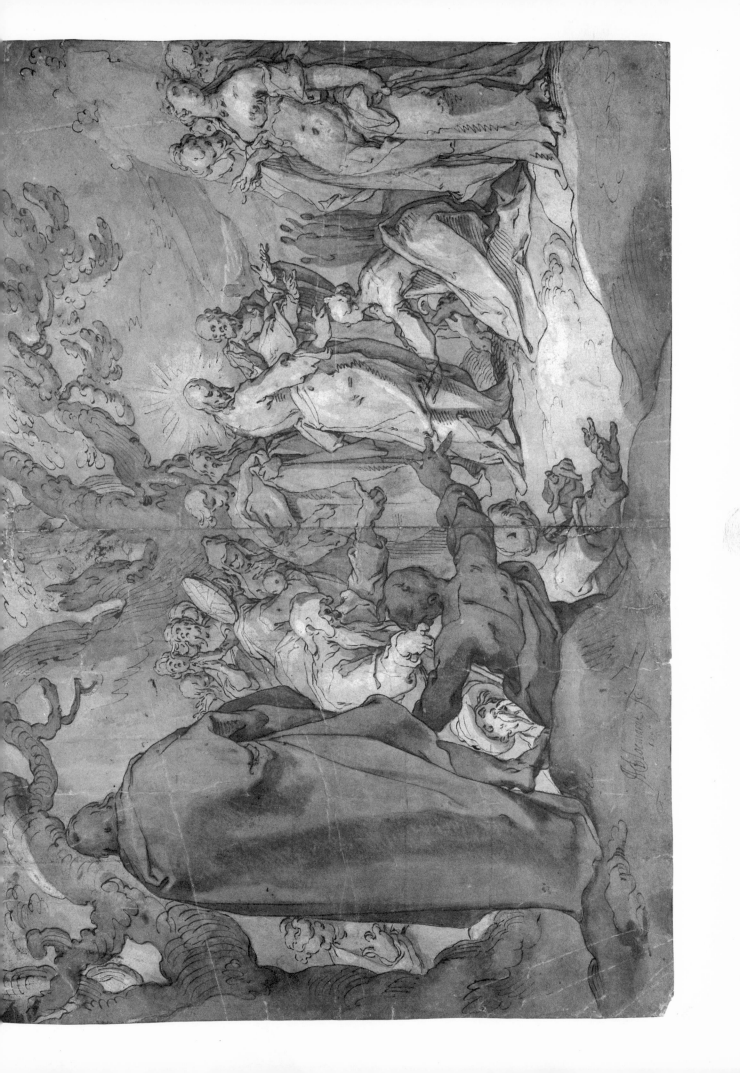

JACQUES DE GHEYN II Antwerp 1565 – The Hague 1629

85 Witches' Sabbath

Pen and brown ink, brown wash, on brownish paper. 9¼ × 14⁷⁄₁₆ in. (23.5 × 36.7 cm.)

Purchase, Joseph Pulitzer Bequest, 62.196

De Gheyn has grouped four witches around a caldron where a ghastly repast is simmering, and into which one of the witches is about to pour a platterful of hearts and bones. A thick greasy cloud of smoke above the pot is suggested by applications of opaque brown wash. This drawing is in De Gheyn's mature style, and his characteristically flexible pen work is at its freest. He treated the ghostly subject in three other drawings. One in the Ashmolean Museum at Oxford is more elaborately finished, and shows three witches gathered around a corpse (ill. J. Q. van Regteren Altena, *Jacques de Gheyn*, Amsterdam, 1935, pl. 7). Another Witches' Sabbath is in Berlin (ill. E. Boch and J. Rosenberg, *Staatliche Museen zu Berlin. Die Niederländischen Meister,* Frankfort-on-the-Main, 1931, no. 3205). A further and now lost drawing is recorded in an engraving by Nicolaes de Clerck (ill. F. W. H. Hollstein, *Dutch and Flemish Etchings, Engravings and Woodcuts ca. 1450–1700*, VII, Amsterdam, n.d., p. 120, no. 96).

PROVENANCE: Hugh N. Squire, London; purchased by the Metropolitan Museum in London in 1962.

BARTHOLOMEUS BREENBERGH
Deventer 1599 – Amsterdam about 1658

86 View of Tivoli

Brush and brown wash. 12⅞ × 17⅟₁₆ in. overall (32.7 × 43.3 cm.) Vertical crease, small tear, and water stain at upper left margin; horizontal crease at bottom of sheet. A portion of the drawing, below the crease, is omitted in the present illustration, which reproduces a surface that measures 11⅜ × 17⅟₁₆ in.

Rogers Fund, 63.2

Breenbergh is known to have been in Rome from 1620 to 1629, and a brilliant series of landscape drawings made in and around the city records his impressions of these years. Our drawing, in which a dark silhouetted foreground so admirably sets off the contrasts of light and transparent shadow in the hills and houses beyond, dates from these Roman years, and very probably is a view of Tivoli. Another view of Tivoli, stylistically very close to the present drawing, is in the Louvre (ill. Frits Lugt, *Musée du Louvre. Dessins des écoles du nord. École hollandaise,* I, Paris, 1929, no. 171, pl. xxv). Further views of Tivoli by Breenbergh are in the British Museum, the Pierpont Morgan Library, and the Crocker Gallery in Sacramento. Breenbergh, one of the many Dutch painters who made their way to Rome in the seventeenth century, was at his best in Italian landscape drawings, and his bold and masterful use of wash to suggest the light and shade of Rome makes him one of the most original of these Italianate draughtsmen.

PROVENANCE: Horace Bolingbroke; sale, London, Sotheby's, June 28, 1962, no. 66; purchased by the Metropolitan Museum in Boston in 1963.

EXHIBITIONS: Ann Arbor, University of Michigan Museum of Art, 1964, Italy through Dutch Eyes. Dutch Seventeenth Century Landscape Artists in Italy, no. 24, ill. pl. xiv and cover.

REMBRANDT HARMENSZ. VAN RIJN
Leyden 1606 – Amsterdam 1669

87   Seated Man Wearing a Flat Cap

Pen and brown ink, brown wash, and white gouache. 5 13/16 × 5 7/16 in. (14.8 × 13.8 cm.)
Bequest of Mrs. H. O. Havemeyer, 29.100.935, The H. O. Havemeyer Collection

Rembrandt has drawn this seated male figure with great authority, enriching the energetic
pen outlines with summary but masterful indications of shadow. This sad-faced man
wearing a broad flat cap, who has cast his coat down beside him on the steps, may be an
actor. Benesch dates the drawing about 1636; at this time Rembrandt made other stylistically comparable drawings of theatrical figures. In a drawing in the Masson Collection at
the École des Beaux-Arts in Paris, a seated male figure, whom Benesch suggests is an actor,
wears a similar flat cap and rests the knuckles of his hand on his knee, as does the model in
the present drawing (ill. Benesch, II, no. 299, fig. 338).

PROVENANCE: Sir Joshua Reynolds (Lugt 2364); Sir Thomas Lawrence (Lugt 2445); William Esdaile (Lugt 2617); Esdaile sale, London, Christie's, June 17, 1840, no. 13; Sir Francis Seymour Haden (Lugt 1227); Haden sale, London, Sotheby's, June 15, 1891, no. 584; H. O. Havemeyer, New York.

BIBLIOGRAPHY: Lippmann, *Rembrandt,* first series, Part III, no. 148b.
Valentiner, *Metropolitan Museum Studies,* III, p. 140, fig. 5.
Ivins, *The Unseen Rembrandt,* pl. 31.
Metropolitan Museum, *European Drawings,* II, ill. no. 8.
Benesch, *Selected Drawings,* pl. 72.
Benesch, II, p. 78, no. 324, fig. 374 (with complete bibliography).

EXHIBITIONS: New York, Metropolitan Museum of Art, 1930, The H. O. Havemeyer Collection, Temporary Exhibition, no. 190.
New York, Pierpont Morgan Library/Cambridge, Fogg Art Museum, 1960, Rembrandt Drawings from American Collections, no. 25, pl. 21 (with complete bibliography).

REMBRANDT HARMENSZ. VAN RIJN
Leyden 1606 – Amsterdam 1669

88   A Cottage among Trees

Pen and brown ink, brown wash, on brownish paper. 6¾ × 10¹³⁄₁₆ in. overall (17.2 × 27.5 cm.)
Vertical strip added to sheet at right and drawing continued in the artist's hand.
Bequest of Mrs. H. O. Havemeyer, 29.100.939, The H. O. Havemeyer Collection

About 1650–1651 Rembrandt, using a fine quill pen, made a series of sharply observed studies of groups of trees, some of them half hiding cottages or barns. What may be the same cottage, surrounded by a meandering fence and standing in a clump of trees, that the artist has recorded in our drawing is studied in a sheet at the Albertina (ill. Benesch, VI, no. 1246, fig. 1470). The latest of the drawings in this group of landscape studies are, as Frits Lugt has pointed out, preparatory for the 1652 etching Clump of Trees with a Vista (ill. Arthur M. Hind, *A Catalogue of Rembrandt's Etchings,* London, 1913, no. 263).

PROVENANCE: Jan Pietersz. Zoomer, Amsterdam; Sir Thomas Lawrence (Lugt 2445); William Esdaile (Lugt 2617); Esdaile sale, London, Christie's, June 17, 1840, no. 119; John Heywood Hawkins (probably Lugt 1472); Hawkins sale, London, Sotheby's, April 29, 1850, no. 1022; Sir Francis Seymour Haden (Lugt 1227); Haden sale, London, Sotheby's, June 15, 1891, no. 587; J.P. Heseltine, London; H. O. Havemeyer, New York.

BIBLIOGRAPHY: Lippmann, *Rembrandt,* first series, Part III, no. 143.
C. Hofstede de Groot, *Die Handzeichnungen Rembrandts,* Haarlem, 1906, no. 1037.
Valentiner, *Metropolitan Museum Studies,* III, fig. 9.
Ivins, *The Unseen Rembrandt,* pl. 35.
Metropolitan Museum, *European Drawings,* II, ill. no. 11.
Tietze, *European Master Drawings,* p. 142, no. 71, ill. p. 143.
Benesch, *Selected Drawings,* no. 174.
Benesch, VI, p. 355, no. 1249, fig. 1475.

EXHIBITIONS: New York, Metropolitan Museum of Art, 1930, The H. O. Havemeyer Collection, Temporary Exhibition, no. 194.
New York, Pierpont Morgan Library/Cambridge, Fogg Art Museum, 1960, Rembrandt Drawings from American Collections, no. 47, pl. 41 (with complete bibliography).

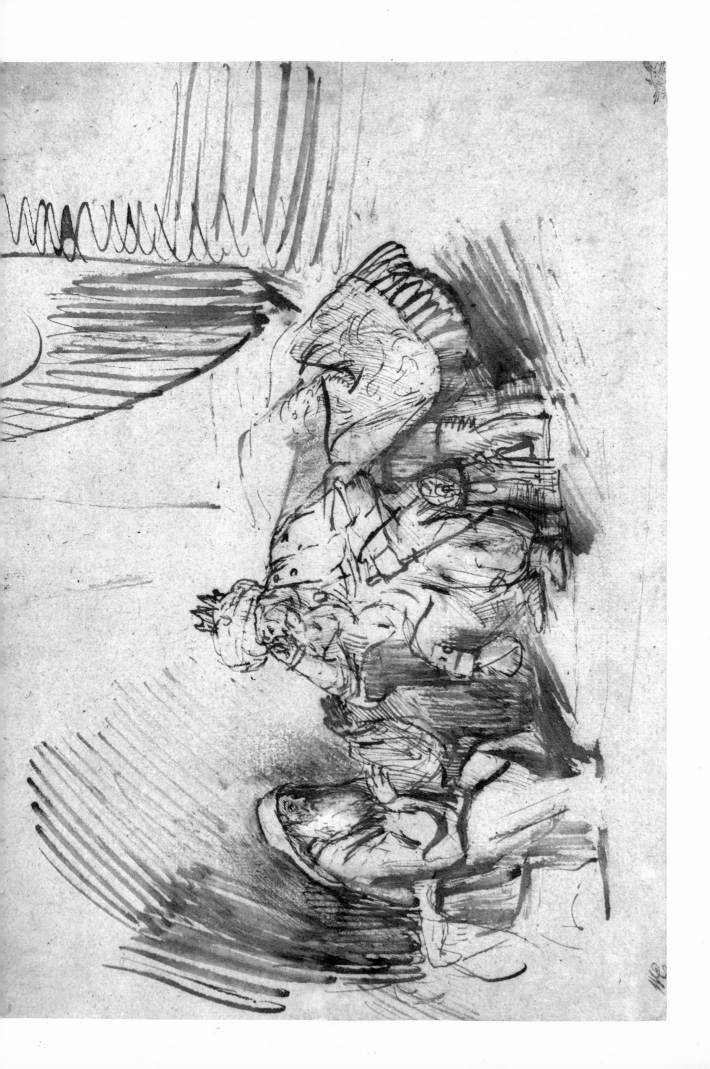

AELBERT CUYP Dordrecht 1620 – Dordrecht 1691

90 Landscape

Yellow and brown water color and gouache over black chalk. 7⁷⁄₁₆ × 12⅛ in. (18.9 × 30.8 cm.)
Rogers Fund, 07.282.13

Cuyp, in his drawings, was a particular master of the art of aerial perspective. The subtle contrast between the shadowed swelling dunes in the foreground and the vast plain swept by changing sea light suggests an almost limitless recession to a transparent horizon. The vertical accent of the church steeple in the middle ground emphasizes the sweep of the plain and establishes the scale of the landscape. It has not been possible to identify the specific place that Cuyp has recorded here, though it must be a view of the plain of Holland from the sea dunes.

PROVENANCE: Freiherr Max von Heyl zu Herrnsheim (Lugt 2879); sale, Stuttgart, H. G. Gutekunst, May 25–26, 1903, no. 108; sale, Amsterdam, Frederik Muller, January 10, 1904, no. 89, ill.; purchased by the Metropolitan Museum in Amsterdam in 1907.

GERBRAND VAN DEN EECKHOUT
Amsterdam 1621 – Amsterdam 1674

91   David's Promise to Bathsheba

Pen and brown ink, brown wash, over black and red chalk. 7⅜ × 10⅝ in. (18.8 × 27 cm.)
Gift of Robert Lehman, 41.187.4

In this exceptionally complete composition drawing Eeckhout represents Bathsheba doing obeisance before King David and interceding for their son Solomon (I Kings 1:15–20). Sumowski has recently pointed out that our drawing is a preparatory study for a picture in a private collection in Hanover, datable 1646. In the Hanover picture the figures of Bathsheba and David appear as they do in this drawing, but the furnishings of the palatial interior differ in detail. In the drawing the king's young mistress Abishag is half hidden behind a twisted column, while in the picture she stands beside David, plumping the pillows of the royal bed. In the Amsterdam print room there is a black and white chalk study by Eeckhout for the figure of King David.

PROVENANCE: Valerius Röver (Lugt 2984c); J. Goll van Franckenstein (Lugt 2987); Jacob de Vos Jacobszoon (Lugt 1450); de Vos sale, Amsterdam, May 22–24, 1883, no. 169; V. Everit Macy, New York; Macy sale, New York, American Art Association, January 6–8, 1938, no. 80, ill.; Robert Lehman, New York.

BIBLIOGRAPHY: Werner Sumowski, "Gerbrand van den Eeckhout als Zeichner," *Oud Holland,* LXXVII, 1962, no. 1, p. 17, ill. p. 15, fig. 10 (the Hanover picture and the Amsterdam drawing also reproduced).

FRANCISCO JOSÉ DE GOYA Y LUCIENTES
Fuendetodos 1746 – Bordeaux 1828

92 Portrait of the Artist

Point of brush and gray wash. 6 × 3 9/16 in. (15.3 × 9.1 cm.)

Signed in point of brush and gray wash on locket pinned to lapel: *Goya;* numbered in pen and dark brown ink at upper right: *1*   Dick Fund, 35.103.1

Goya reveals in this small and powerful self-portrait, executed with the point of a brush, a technical virtuosity that was later to enable him to dash off an extraordinary series of miniatures on ivory. The artist, who wears at his lapel a locket inscribed with his name, stares at the spectator with an intensity that suggests that the portrait is a mirror image. The drawing, which Wehle dates about 1795, when Goya was forty-nine, figures as the first page of an album of fifty Goya drawings purchased by the Metropolitan Museum in 1935. The album, containing drawings dating from several periods of the artist's activity, had been made up by his son or grandson and sold to Valentín Carderera, a Spanish painter and man of letters who at one time owned some four hundred of Goya's drawings. From Carderera the album passed to Federico de Madrazo, then to Mariano Fortuny y de Madrazo, from whom it was acquired by the Metropolitan Museum. In addition to the self-portrait, the three other Goya drawings reproduced in this volume formed part of the Metropolitan's Carderera-Fortuny album.

PROVENANCE: Valentín Carderera, Madrid; Federico de Madrazo, Madrid; Mariano Fortuny y de Madrazo, Venice; purchased by the Metropolitan Museum in Paris in 1935.

BIBLIOGRAPHY: Carderera, *Gazette des Beaux-Arts*, pp. 222–227.
V. von Loga, "Drei Briefe Goyas," *Kunst und Künstler,* VI, 1908, ill. p. 65.
Wehle, *Fifty Drawings by Goya,* p. 7, ill. frontispiece.

EXHIBITIONS: Paris, Bibliothèque Nationale, 1935, Goya, no. 297.
New York, Metropolitan Museum of Art, 1936, Francisco Goya. His Paintings, Drawings and Prints, no. 19, ill.

FRANCISCO JOSÉ DE GOYA Y LUCIENTES
Fuendetodos 1746 – Bordeaux 1828

93   The Swing

Brush and gray wash. 9⁵⁄₁₆ × 5¾ in. (23.6 × 14.5 cm.)

Numbered in brush and gray wash at upper right: *21*; in pen and dark brown ink at upper right: *2*

Verso: Brush and gray wash study of a standing maja and an officer. Numbered in brush and gray wash at upper left: *22*; in pen and dark brown ink at upper right: *3*

Dick Fund, 35.103.2

This lively sketch, where brush and transparent gray washes are used by Goya with marvelous ease and authority, is part of a group of drawings known as the Madrid and sometimes as the Large Sanlúcar sketchbook, begun probably at the country estate of the Duchess of Alba at Sanlúcar near Cadiz, and finished in Madrid in 1797. The page numbers on drawings from this now dismembered volume run up to ninety-four, but only sixty-six drawings (or thirty-three sheets, for Goya made drawings on both recto and verso) that certainly were part of the volume can today be identified. The Metropolitan Museum possesses sixteen of these drawings. Some ten years earlier Goya had treated the theme of the present drawing in one of the seven large decorative paintings commissioned by the Duchess of Osuna for the Alameda, her country residence near Madrid. In the canvas for the Alameda the lady on the swing has her skirts tied modestly above her slippers, while in our drawing they are free to reveal trim ankles. Miss Sayre has suggested Goya's anecdotal intention by entitling the drawing: "Gallant shocked by a girl wearing Spanish dress because she has not tied down her skirts when swinging."

PROVENANCE: Valentín Carderera, Madrid; Federico de Madrazo, Madrid; Mariano Fortuny y de Madrazo, Venice; purchased by the Metropolitan Museum in Paris in 1935.

BIBLIOGRAPHY: Carderera, *Gazette des Beaux-Arts*, pp. 222–227.
Wehle, *Fifty Drawings by Goya*, pl. III.
José López-Rey, *Goya's Caprichos. Beauty, Reason, and Caricature*, Princeton, 1953, I, p. 30; II, fig. 21.
Stoll, *Goya. Dessins*, p. 12, pl. 3.
Eleanor A. Sayre, "Eight Books of Drawings by Goya—I," *Burlington Magazine*, CVI, January 1964, p. 27, fig. 16.

EXHIBITIONS: Paris, Bibliothèque Nationale, 1935, Goya, no. 297.
New York, Metropolitan Museum of Art, 1936, Francisco Goya. His Paintings, Drawings and Prints, no. 20, ill.

FRANCISCO JOSÉ DE GOYA Y LUCIENTES
Fuendetodos 1746 – Bordeaux 1828

94 Crowd in a Park

Brush and brown wash; border drawn in brush and the same brown wash. 8⅛ × 5⅝ in. (20.6 × 14.3 cm.)

Numbered in pen or brush and pale brown ink at upper right: *31*(?); in pen and dark brown ink at upper right: *19*.   Dick Fund, 35.103.19

Stylistic evidence and the testimony of Valentín Carderera, who probably had received his information from Goya's son or grandson, concur in assigning a group of brush drawings executed by Goya in a dark brown, probably sepia, wash to the year 1819. The Metropolitan Museum possesses twenty-nine of the drawings in this so-called Sepia-Wash Series, and more than twenty further sheets can be identified in other collections. The subjects treated by Goya in this group of drawings are only occasionally brutal and violent; the peaceful pleasures of Spanish life are the theme of many of the designs. As Wehle put it: "The out-raged social reporter turns away from the horrors of famine, war, and imprisonment." The present drawing representing a holiday crowd gathered on a meadow recalls the festive pastoral themes of Goya's early paintings, particularly the Pradera de San Isidro of 1788 in the Prado, where the artist represented a host of Madrileños gathered on a plain outside the city to celebrate the feast of San Isidro.

PROVENANCE: Valentín Carderera, Madrid; Federico de Madrazo, Madrid; Mariano Fortuny y de Madrazo, Venice; purchased by the Metropolitan Museum in Paris in 1935.

BIBLIOGRAPHY: Carderera, *Gazette des Beaux-Arts*, pp. 222–227.
Wehle, *Fifty Drawings by Goya,* pl. XXI.
Metropolitan Museum, *European Drawings,* II, ill. no. 22.
Stoll, *Goya. Dessins,* p. 27, pl. 44.

EXHIBITIONS: Paris, Bibliothèque Nationale, 1935, Goya, no. 297.
New York, Metropolitan Museum of Art, 1936, Goya. His Paintings, Drawings and Prints, no. 25, ill.

FRANCISCO JOSÉ DE GOYA Y LUCIENTES
Fuendetodos 1746 – Bordeaux 1828

95 Nun Frightened by a Ghost

Brush and two tones of brown wash. 8⅟₁₆ × 5¹¹⁄₁₆ in. (20.5 × 14.4 cm.)

Numbered in pen and brown ink at upper right: *65*(?); in pen and darker brown ink at upper
    right: *37*.

Dick Fund, 35.103.37

Goya represents a terrified nun awakened by the nightmare vision of a hideous serenading
monk. The contrast between the dark washes used in the foreground to describe the nun's
habit and the lighter tones that indicate the guitar-playing friar does much to suggest a distinction between reality and hallucination. The satirical intention of this drawing, which is
part of the so-called Sepia-Wash Series of 1819, is not explicit; perhaps Goya is not so much
recording the torments of an anguished penitent as mocking a certain tradition of Spanish
mysticism by replacing a nocturnal angel musician with the sinister strumming monk.

PROVENANCE: Valentín Carderera, Madrid; Federico de Madrazo, Madrid; Mariano Fortuny y de Madrazo,
    Venice; purchased by the Metropolitan Museum in Paris in 1935.

BIBLIOGRAPHY: Carderera, *Gazette des Beaux-Arts*, pp. 222–227.
Wehle, *Fifty Drawings by Goya*, pl. XXXV.
Metropolitan Museum, *European Drawings*, II, ill. no. 26.

EXHIBITIONS: Paris, Bibliothèque Nationale, 1935, Goya, no. 297.
New York, Metropolitan Museum of Art, 1936, Francisco Goya. His Paintings, Drawings and
    Prints, no. 31, ill.

PABLO PICASSO born Málaga 1881

96 Nude Woman

Charcoal. 19⅟₁₆ × 12⁵⁄₁₆ in. (48.4 × 31.3 cm.)

Charcoal inscription on verso in the artist's hand: *49 bis Picasso*

The Alfred Stieglitz Collection, 49.70.34

This rigorously constructed cubist figure drawing dates from the spring of 1910, and was exhibited in New York the following year by Alfred Stieglitz in Picasso's first one-man show in America. The exhibition at Stieglitz's in 1911 seems, furthermore, to have been the first time any works by Picasso had been exhibited in this country. Alfred Barr has very aptly said of the present drawing that "the effect might be compared to a geometrized anatomical chart in which transparent cross sections of the body are superimposed on the silhouette," and he adds that "Apollinaire, the chief defender of cubism, wrote in 1913 of Picasso 'assassinating' anatomy with the science and technique of a great surgeon."

PROVENANCE: Alfred Stieglitz, New York.

BIBLIOGRAPHY: *Camera Work,* no. XXXVI, 1911, ill. opp. p. 70; also ill. in special numbers of 1912 and 1913.
Zervos, *Picasso,* II, Part 1, no. 208, ill. p. 103.
Barr, *Picasso,* pp. 72–73, ill. p. 72.

EXHIBITIONS: New York, Photo-Secession Gallery, 1911, Early and Recent Drawings by Pablo Picasso of Paris.
New York, Sixty-Ninth Regimental Armory, 1913, International Exhibition of Modern Art, probably no. 351.
New York, Museum of Modern Art, 1939–1940, Picasso, Forty Years of his Art, no. 92.
New York, Museum of Modern Art/Chicago, Art Institute, 1957, Picasso, 75th Anniversary Exhibition, p. 39, ill.
Rotterdam/Paris/New York, 1958–1959, From Clouet to Matisse. French Drawings from American Collections, no. 216, pl. 216 (with complete list of previous exhibitions).

THOMAS GAINSBOROUGH Sudbury 1727 – London 1788

98 Landscape

Charcoal, estompe, heightened with white chalk, on blue paper. 10 9/16 × 13 1/4 in. (26.8 × 33.3 cm.)

Inscription on verso in Esdaile's hand: *1824 W E - Nassau's sale NN 57 x Gainsboro*

Rogers Fund, 07.283.5

It seems probable that this landscape improvisation dates from the time of Gainsborough's residence in Bath (1759–1774). In his early years in Suffolk he had gained such a mastery of notation after nature that by the 1760s he could launch into inventive landscape, create a convincing vista with the broadest strokes of black chalk. The compositional formula employed in this design goes back to Claude Lorrain, so much admired in eighteenth century England. A stretch of water leads the eye diagonally into the composition, a single silhouetted tree establishes the middle ground, and the castle-crowned hill in the left background is balanced by the mass of trees on the right. Miss Woodall has called attention to a passage in Edward Edwards's *Anecdotes of Painters* (London, 1808), where Gainsborough's drawings of the Bath period are neatly characterized: "After he settled at Bath . . . he adopted a very different manner, both of style and execution, the subjects being more romantic in their composition and their execution more indeterminate and (if the expression be allowed) more licentious. . . . They were executed by a process rather capricious, truly deserving the epithet bestowed upon them by a witty lady who called them 'moppings.' Many of these were in black and white, which colours were applied in the following manner: a small bit of sponge tied to a bit of stick served as a pencil for the shadows, and a small lump of whiting held by a pair of tongs was the instrument with which the high lights were applied." The Metropolitan Museum possesses another similar charcoal and white chalk landscape drawing from the Bath period (07.283.6).

PROVENANCE: George Nassau; Nassau sale, London, March 25–27, 1824, probably part of no. 244; William Esdaile (Lugt 2617); purchased by the Metropolitan Museum in London in 1907.

BIBLIOGRAPHY: Mary Woodall, *Gainsborough's Landscape Drawings,* London, 1939, pp. 52, 142, no. 465. Metropolitan Museum, *European Drawings,* II, ill. no. 58.

INDEX

Designed by Peter Oldenburg. Composed in English Monotype Garamond by Clarke & Way, Inc., and printed on Mohawk Superfine Text by The Meriden Gravure Company. Bound in Columbia Riverside Linen, with endpapers of Curtis Tweedweave Text, by the Russell-Rutter Co., Inc.